Ellie's Golden Fables

Written by Ellie Adel

Illustrated by Danielle Kluth

Published by

MELROSE BOOKS

An Imprint of Melrose Press Limited
St Thomas Place, Ely
Cambridgeshire
CB7 4GG, UK
www.melrosebooks.co.uk

FIRST EDITION

Copyright © Ellie Adel 2012

The Author asserts her moral right to
be identified as the author of this work

Cover designed by Jeremy Kay

ISBN 978-1-907732-78-2

Printed and bound in Great Britain by:
Mimeo Ltd, Huntingdon, Cambridgeshire

FSC
www.fsc.org
MIX
Paper from
responsible sources
FSC® C019549

DEDICATION

I dedicate this book to my loving, kind and caring mother who ever remains in my memory, and to my three daughters whose nurturing love and care resurrected me from near death.

Individually these four women have a special place in my heart. Each in their own way is a true example of a New Age child of Mother Earth.

The writing of this book was inspired by the creativity of my third daughter during time I spent with her in Maleny, Queensland, in 1991.

E. A.

Dear Friend,

We are alive and living during a time of great change on Earth. Everything is changing. Earth herself is changing and so, indeed, is time.

When it comes to humans coping with change, most of us are totally unprepared and ill-equipped to handle it, especially when it comes unexpectedly into our lives.

For the last 2000 years there has been great ignorance or darkness of spirit on Earth. During that time there has been much illusion and disillusion, false hope and false belief. It is difficult for the majority of us to recognize and realize this and to break out of our old conditioned patterns of the past.

The spirit within Earth and all things of the Earth has been dormant, negatively active, or sleeping while the Piscean Age has been upon us. That time is passing and the living spirit within all is beginning to awaken and become conscious of itself. This is causing tremendous stress, chaos and upheaval in the lives of those who are unaware of what is happening. Nothing can prevent the awakening of spirit on Earth because nothing or no one on Earth can stay time. The living spirit within all things is destined to waken and it is time it did so.

Many are fighting with crazed frenzy, stubbornly hanging on to their old way of life. They cling with determination to outmoded traditions and beliefs as, dogmatically, they struggle to maintain the past. It cannot be maintained. Time will not allow it. The new Aquarian Age has dawned. We can't turn back the hands of time.

It is time false hopes, disillusionment and ignorance were dissolved and our spirits set free. It is time for New Age consciousness. It truly is a time for rejoicing, not for shedding tears.

These fables have been written at this specific point in time to assist those who are destined to transform or heal themselves by consciously creating change in the physical body by the spirit within.

It is my greatest wish to assist any who are struggling helplessly against the tide of change to go with the flow. I am well acquainted with the pain and suffering that ignorant victims of time have forced upon them. I have been an inflicted victim myself.

These fables have been written not by me but through me. I have merely been the medium or the instrument which held the pen. I'm certain there is no person small enough to believe discrimination of sex is intended when the word 'Man' is used in abbreviation of human and humanity or 'he/she' is used instead of the name of a living creature.

To be unaffected by time and its subsequent changes it is essential we have true self-awareness. It was a wise person indeed who wrote the words 'know yourself'. The intention of these fables is to help those, whose time has come, to know themselves. Their intention is not to shock or offend. If, by any means, the fables have come into your possession, know it is not coincidence: it is time you began to know yourself.

I believe that we as individuals can effectively create change for the betterment of ourselves, our nation and our planet when the creative spirit within is conscious and active.

Fear not the spirit within yourself awakening. There is nothing to fear or worry about. It is love and compassion that activates or triggers spirit into wakefulness and activity. It is rejection or loss of loved ones which causes it to close down, become depressed, inactive or negatively creative.

It was with love and compassion that these fables were given to me, and it is with love and compassion that I pass them on to you. Please accept them in the context they are written, despite any misgivings or wonder you may have regarding their writing, and allow the dormant or unconscious spirit within yourself to gently awaken.

Nothing can prevent progression of time, evolution of consciousness, and the awakening of the human spirit.

Mother Earth is patiently waiting to also be given love, compassion and caring. It is necessary every single one of us give her these things if she is to survive time and the awakening of her inner spirit.

Sincerely,

Ellie Adel

CONTENTS

ILLUSTRATIONS

AUSTRALIA'S ANIMALS

I AM THE SPIRIT OF AUSTRALIA'S ANIMALS.

All animals natural to Australia are of the vibration of service. They were created by the Creator of All to reflect the nature of Australia's people. Most of Australia's animals are of a timid nature. Few Australian people realize they are creatures of habit.

Animals of a timid nature are never aggressive unless they experience great provocation. Australia's people enjoy provocation. They delight in undermining the confidence of their fellow Australians. They enjoy seeing their mates squirm with embarrassment, and they enjoy provoking timid souls until they react in aggravation. All of Australia's animals will bite or scratch if provoked, as will the people of Australia. It is time this provocation ceased.

I will tell you of an animal of Australia that was most placid and why he was so placid. In the beginning, when all animals were created, there was one which had more initiative and enterprise than the rest. That one was called The Ambassador. He was rather like a large dog but he had feathers. Those feathers were a combination of all colours. The birds of the air and animals of the land admired and respected him. He always behaved in an exemplary manner.

One day he did something totally out of character with himself. He snarled. This quite shocked those who lived in proximity to him. In fact he was quite shocked by his own new behaviour. He did not feel happy with himself when he made the snarling sound. He then discovered that when he snarled, his friends withdrew from his company. Being a friendly and compassionate creature he could not understand why, when he made the new sound, his companions withdrew. To regain their friendship he snarled louder and longer in an effort to gain their attention. The more he snarled, the more he was rejected. The more rejected he became, the more he snarled. In anger he began to tear out his beautiful coloured feathers.

His appearance began to change. He grew short hair where once he had displayed coloured feathers. His mouth began to hang open and he began to develop fangs. He snarled and spat at all who came within his presence, and the more he did, the uglier his appearance became.

There was one small creature that defended the devolving animal. That one could communicate with all creatures. That one was a frog, a green frog. Frog knew well what it felt like to change one's character and form, and he explained to the fanged, hairy one that when there is peace within, it is possible to live in harmony with all living creatures. The hairy one never realized he had been responsible for creating disharmony by snarling, and he began to follow the small one's advice.

At first he was to smile. This was quite difficult because his mouth fanged open. Next he was to purr instead of snarl. This was not easy to do either, but as I said in the beginning, the Ambassador had initiative and enterprise. With the help of his green friend he smiled more and snarled less. The animals of the land and the birds of the air came closer and closer, and as they did he felt a great peace within. He loved their companionship and patted the young on the head.

A strange thing began to happen. The claws he possessed began to fade and he began to grow finger-like protrusions. He became more and more gentle and passive. He began to sleep for long periods of time and to eat less. While asleep, he made loud purring sounds, and his need to sleep was respected. While asleep, feathers began to replace the stringy hair, but instead of being feathers of many colours, they were white. They were so white they glowed in the dark. Whenever there was a dispute among the animals or the birds, they would awaken the Illumined One, and he, with his wisdom, solved the problem.

The people who dwelt on the land loved and respected him. He could communicate with all living creatures of Australia. He dwelt in peace and harmony for aeons of time.

As time went on, the people and the creatures of Earth began to snarl and spit and bite and scratch. Our glowing hero was horrified by what he saw. He well knew the consequence of that behaviour, and instead of sleeping he spent more time awake, trying to teach the snarling, spitting, biting, scratching ones to change their ways. None would listen. In desperation he called on the Great White Spirit of Australia to stop the devolution of Australia's beautiful creatures. He asked the Great Spirit to keep Australia's animals gentle and peaceful, and in return he would become extinct. His wish was granted. He became extinct, and Australia's animals roamed the continent. They were timid, shy but friendly creatures. They mirrored the people of the land.

There has been great provocation in the lives of Australia's people in recent centuries. There also has been great provocation in the lives of the animals of the land, the birds of the air, and the fish in the sea by the people.

It is time the people were told the story of the Dodo and why he became extinct. The native people of this country had a different name for Dodo. They called him Bunyip. Although the Great White Spirit released that wise one from the Earth, he did not die. He became immortal because the service he gave to his fellows was exemplary. He gave himself to benefit those he loved and cared for.

This message comes to you through me, the Spirit of Australia's animals, from Bunyip, or if you prefer, the Dodo. This immortal one says listen to the green ones. They speak truth. If you wish to have peace, love and harmony in your life, be kind, be gentle and serve your fellow man, and by doing so you will become immortal and live among the stars as I do.

I am the Spirit of Australia's animals.

ECHIDNA

I AM THE SPIRIT OF ECHIDNA.

I am of the vibration of truth. Echidna is a creation of the eternal living God. This One created all animals. Every creation of God is of a particular vibration. Each country has a particular vibration, therefore certain animals are native to certain countries. Echidna is native to Australia. Australia is a separated country but soon she will begin to slowly drift north. She will, with time, return to her home, or where she began. When separation occurred, it was necessary she have animals to reflect to her the truth of her being. Echidna was the first animal created to reflect Australia.

Echidna is a quiet but purposeful animal. He goes about life in a practical manner. If there is cause for alarm, he tenses his body and, as he does, the spines that are part of his makeup stand erect. Tenseness is constant in Echidna. Instinctively he knows he carries the truth of Australia, and is very protective.

When Echidna is hungry he will brook no interference. He has an incredible sense of smell. He lives on ants and can smell an ant nest from a great distance. Echidna is friendly with all native animals but most wary of humans. Instinctively he knows humans have caused the separation between God and all things.

Echidna lives in harmony with nature. He is an animal of patience. He can survive without eating for great lengths of time, but when he decides to eat, he will devour enormous quantities of ants. Echidna is the enemy of all ants. He has a long tongue which laps them up. He does not have taste buds; he simply laps them up and swallows them. When he has sufficiently indulged himself, he curls up and goes to sleep.

Truth is ever constant. What is, is. The spiny one lives this. He is an anteater, and he contains the essence of the One God. Wherever he goes, he is protected. The exception is Man and his appendages. No native animal will ever harm an echidna. Most echidnas live alone and live to an old age.

The spirit of Echidna is a delightful one. Echidna can be playful with young creatures of the wild. Bandicoots love him, especially the young. They will scamper about him, and in his friendly way he will teach them truth of the spirit within themselves. He does this by play-acting.

Echidna is a great actor and when on stage he is an uproarious success. He can imitate sounds of other animals and mimic some birds. He can even play the part of an ant. He is well qualified to play this role as he has observed them all of his life. By mimicking the animals, he reflects the truth or essence of their own creation.

Man has no idea of the truth of Echidna. Echidna hides the truth. Man sees himself because Echidna also mimics Man. Man sees the spiny one on guard, with his spines erect and protective of himself. This is the truth of Man today. He is ever on guard and protective of what he believes is his.

Echidna, although friendly with all native animals, has one true friend. That one is Unicorn. Because Echidna is an animal of truth, he can and does frequent a higher dimension. He is at home in this other dimension. In fact, he prefers to be there. He goes to this other dimension when he sleeps, and that is how sometimes he is caught unaware and drowns. He must return to this dimension to eat and give truth to other animals.

Unicorn reflects Echidna. All creatures of God must have another creature to mirror truth to them. Unicorn mirrors all highly evolved animals. Each country has a native animal that reflects truth to other animals.

All of God's creatures depend on other creatures to survive. This is part of the plan of creation. Echidna depends on ants for his survival.

Ants know this and unconsciously accept their fate. They do not suffer in their demise. With Echidna their fate is quick.

Echidna fears facing the truth of himself, as do all living creatures. Both animals and humans fear acceptance of self.

Echidna, although he constantly returns to the dimension of spirit in sleep, has difficulty in getting to sleep. His spines prevent him from sleeping comfortably. He can curl up into a small ball when he relaxes, and sleep peacefully. His spirit will then leave him and go play with unicorns. When he is relaxed he can sleep for long periods of time. He only wakens when it is necessary he eat to survive in the Earthly dimension.

Echidna has small, beadlike eyes. These eyes miss nothing. He is ever on the watch to incorporate something new into his acting repertoire. Young animals prod him when asleep. He will waken to their prods and perform for them because he must ever reflect truth to the native animals.

If Man could only realize Echidna mirrors truth, he would dislike what he has become and want to change. As Man evolves he will learn to relax. He will not be so tense, so sharp, so spiny. There will be no need for him to be protective. When this happens, Man will frequent the spiritual dimension as does Echidna, and Unicorn will reflect him.

When Man's Earthly learning has been accomplished, the native animals will have completed their Earthly cycle and all will return home to the realm of spirit.

I am the Spirit of Echidna.

KOOKABURRA

AM THE SPIRIT OF KOOKABURRA.

I love to laugh. Kookaburras are delightful creatures. Of all the birds of the air, kookaburras are most akin to Man in nature.

Kookaburra is bright of eye and quick with beak. He can sum up a situation in the wink of an eye. To be a kookaburra is a great privilege. One is of the spirit or nature of air. When there is air, there is life. Without air to breathe there would be no life on Earth.

Back in the time of long ago, Kookaburra held precedence over the birds because he had common sense. By common sense I refer to God-given sense. His senses were highly developed, much more so than other birds. He had the ability to integrate the senses into one sense. That sense is what is known as common sense.

There is nothing common about common sense. Believe me, common creatures rarely possess common sense. However, I will continue the story of Kookaburra. Because of his common or integrated senses he developed a higher sense. This sense is sometimes referred to as the third eye. Kookaburra does not have to leave his perch to know what's happening in the world around him. He does not even have to open his eyes to see. He sees from within. Because of his common sense Kookaburra can sense when there is danger, he can sense when there is to be rain, and he can sense when the dawn of the sun is approaching. Kookaburras can be likened to alarm clocks. Whenever you hear a kookaburra, he is signalling something is about to happen. He can sense it with his common sense.

Kookaburras of today still maintain a vestige of their original common sense, but the old day's Kooka is gone. I will tell you a story that will surely bring you to your senses.

In the beginning, when all was new, all that had been created was at its most glorious. All was in harmony and there was perfect peace. Every animal, every bird, every fish, every flower, everything was perfect. Ah, I remember it well. There was love, co-ordination and co-operation. The sun shone warmly and the moon was new. The elements of Earth were delightful vibrations to know. We had many a laugh together. We were all young spirits then. We accepted who and what we were and who and what our fellow creatures were. We knew we were all different but we delighted in our difference.

I spent many an hour endeavouring to teach Crocodile to laugh. He'd open his jaws and throw his head back in glee, but to this day a crocodile cannot laugh. My laugh was exclusively mine. I was created the vibration of laughter. I was created to reflect common sense. It is common sense to laugh. Laughter dispels fear, it dispels confusion, it breaks all barriers; it can even transcend time. It is able to do this because it is a higher sense.

But enough of this. Let me get back to the beginning.

After a time we all tired of our uniqueness. We actually became tired of being who and what we were. We wanted and longed to be something altogether different. This, in a sense, led to our downfall. We began to find fault with each other and ourselves. Some birds actually plucked out their own beautiful coloured feathers. I myself am guilty of that. You may find it hard to believe that, in the beginning, I was a bird of brilliant hues. I was of the colour of shining copper interlaced with azure blue and green. Ah, I do regret my past actions. They are not to be laughed at.

Time began to weigh heavy on us. We became bored with the idyllic existence we lived. What fools we were. Some of us began to wander in search of adventure and then the bickering began. It began with the birds. I'm sure it was the fault of the element of air. Air became unsettled and blew up a storm. None of us had ever seen a storm before. We'd only experienced light, cooling breezes.

Air blew in rain like we'd never seen. It was continuous. The sun became sulky and refused to shine, and the spirit—of the land, and within us all—developed self-will. There became great disorder and it led to chaos. Of course this took millions and millions of Earth years. I have lost my sense of time these days.

Back in the old days the only time I wasn't laughing was when I was eating. All used to tell me I even chuckled and cackled in my sleep. Today I only laugh when there is something to laugh at. I even look for things not to laugh at. Isn't that a sad state for a kookaburra to be in? I have become quite petulant in my old age. I prefer to think of the past and how it used to be.

People of today are the same as me. It's not that they don't know how to laugh, it's just that they have separated senses. Their common sense isn't there any more and it can never come back while they live in the past.

Every now and then I feel like exploding into a great burst of laughter and I do, just to know I still am of the vibration of laughter, but none share my mirth. Today people snigger and laugh behind doors. They talk about and criticize each other, and are dissatisfied with what they have and who they are. Today people are trying so hard to be what they are not. I can sense this and it is not good.

Laughter is the solution to many life problems. A laugh a day keeps the doctor away. I shall teach you how to laugh. I want to laugh and I want to laugh now. I want to live now because that is where I am: now. I am not living in the time of long ago. I am living now.

When people accept they are who they are, they can live in the now. Whilever people want other than what they have, they cannot live in the now. They are struggling to live in the future. It is not difficult to be yourself; at least it wasn't in the old days. I want to be me!

Now I have told you the story of Kookaburra, I beg you to accept and be content with yourself. When you do this, those in association with you will do the same. The animals will feel your contentment and they in turn will relax and become content. The birds of the air will follow suit. When there is no bickering, air will calm down and the other elements will comply. I can feel a laugh coming on at the thought of it all. Open your mouth with me, throw back your head and let the sound rush out. Bend over and laugh. Stand up and laugh. Sit and laugh. Roll on the ground and laugh. Wherever you are, whatever you are doing, throw your head back and laugh, and as you do your senses will unite and you'll be of the vibration of common sense. You'll be you.

I am the Light of Kookaburra.

TURTLE

 AM THE SPIRIT OF TURTLE.

Turtles come in many colours, but the message I bring this day is the story of the green turtle.

Turtles are sea creatures. They also frequent the land. Turtles live for many years. During their life they grow in consciousness, as does Man.

Man goes to sea in ships but Turtle takes his home to sea. This is the difference between Man and Turtle. Man leaves his home to go to sea.

In the time of long ago, turtles had no shell. They lived on the land and frolicked in the sea. They were sensitive creatures. Their skin was tender as was their heart. They trusted all living creatures, and because they had trust in the generosity and goodwill of others they lived a good life.

There was one turtle that was more adventurous than the rest. He liked to travel further when on the land and swim deeper when in the sea. Eventually he became separated from his companions. His life began to change. He associated with creatures unknown to the family of turtles. These creatures enjoyed rough and tumble games, and our lone turtle found he was vulnerable and prone to accident. Where once he had complete trust in his companions, he began to lose trust because they seemed to not care about him and his sensitivity to being hurt.

He wanted to participate in their way of life, but if he was to do so he knew he had to protect himself. He joined in the rough and tumble games less and began to procrastinate by himself. His nature became quite crusty, and as it did he began to develop an outer crust. This crust became thicker and heavier as time went on. He found it adequately protected him from those who were insensitive to his gentleness, but it was cumbersome. It took him longer to travel the land and to reach the sea. He became a frustrated creature. He neither belonged to the land nor to the sea. He realized not that the hard shell he carried on his back was of his own making, he just knew he was a prisoner within himself.

The heavier he became, the more difficult it was for him to move, until one day he could not move. Tears rolled from his sad, lonely eyes. Have you ever seen a turtle cry? There is nothing more heart-breaking than the tears of a turtle. That one was far from his family and he scarcely remembered them, when into his vision crawled a long-forgotten sight. It was a turtle without a shell and he was most inquisitive. He gazed with recognition and sadness into the tear-filled eyes of the old one. The old one implored the young one to return to his family, but the young one was eager for adventure and continued on his way.

With resignation the old one closed his eyes and fell asleep. He dreamed of a place where all was green. There was peace, there was harmony, and there were turtles. They meandered among the greenness with love and trust, with no crusty shell on their backs.

The young turtle that had gone adventuring heeded the old tur-tle's warning. Returning, he approached the old one and was amazed to discover his shell had turned green. He tried to awaken the old turtle but he had died in his sleep.

It is sad that Man, like the turtle, has the need to protect himself from the pain his companions inflict. It is sad that Man knows not his own sensitivity.

Those who today travel the land in search of adventure, or sail or swim the waters of the deep, are like the turtle of old. They are searching and seeking for what they know not. In time they will all long to return home. Home is where the pastures are green. Home is where the heart is. Home is where there is generosity and trust.

In any land that is green its inhabitants may sleep soundly, and when the time comes to leave Earthly existence they may pass into another dimension with perfect love and trust.

Turtles exist today and they are multiplying in numbers. This is because Man's nature has become crustier and crustier. There are, however, fewer green turtles than there are other coloured turtles because there are fewer people of the vibration of green.

Man reflects his environment. Green the environment and Man will see more green turtles. When Man frees himself of his crusty nature and gives service to the animals of the land and the sea, the shells of turtles again become soft.

The green turtle today fears Man. He lives in dark green waters and dislikes coming ashore.

These turtles certainly do exist and they exist in Australian waters.

I am the Spirit of Turtle.

DOLPHIN

AM THE SPIRIT OF DOLPHIN.

To invoke the dolphin is to invoke the vibration of creativity. The dolphin is a creator of light. Dolphin is an acrobat, he is a comedian, he is a lover of laughter. Wherever there is laughter, there is creative spirit.

When Dolphin was created in the time of long ago, he was a splendid creation. The lines and contours of his body were magnificent. He was designed to reflect the light of the sun and the spirit or essence of the water. He would leap high in an effort to reach the sun, and he would dive deep, endeavouring to touch the very soul of his mother, the ocean.

Dolphin today is still a magnificent specimen of living creation but the light has dimmed within him throughout time. Dolphins of old could leap sixty feet into the air, and as they leapt they performed their own show. They were the actors of the waters of Earth. They would twist and turn their bodies in exquisite movement. They created joy and delighted all with their playful, happy antics. Always their performance was timed to catch the rays of the sun on their glistening, wet bodies. The sun and the water were their playfellows. Water sprites laughed with glee and sunbeams shone with exuberance. It delights my heart to think of olden times.

Dolphin pods were large and many, and when whole families displayed their talent the angels in heaven wept with joy. Heaven and Earth were one in those days. All dimensions of Earth were one. There was no separation. There was no time.

The waters of Mother Earth waved and bobbed to each other as gentle sea breezes floated past. The only sounds to be heard were the sounds of happiness and laughter.

It was destined in the plan of creation that all love, truth and happiness be lost then rediscovered. When one is given anything freely it is rarely appreciated or valued. The Creator of All gave the gift of life. Those who have life rarely appreciate that gift until they begin to lose it.

Dolphin of old loved life. He knew he could create as he himself had been created. With the rays of the sun and the bubbling playfulness of the water he would create colour designs in the air, and laugh and laugh with pleasure at his own creativity.

Dolphin of today loves still to create. He loves to create happiness but most of all he loves to create and hear laughter. He can sense when there is unhappiness and tries his hardest to create smiles. Instinctively he knows a smile will turn into a laugh, and when he hears laughter he will perform even harder.

There are many performers in human form today. They don't perform to create joy and laughter. They perform for their own aggrandizement. They are conceited and arrogant. They are performers much different to Dolphin. Their performance gives no pleasure, it gives no happiness; it creates big waves, and the sun does not shine in the lives of those around them. The angels in heaven weep for them. They weep with unhappiness and sadness, and those in the dimension of conceit and arrogance know not the hurt they cause to all who love them. Conceit and arrogance are always accompanied by the inability to create. Pomposity exists on Earth today like never before.

The great dolphin pods of old no longer exist. Dolphins of today enjoy company and are rarely seen alone. Dolphins of today display still their talent, but it is only the creatively-orientated who enjoy and appreciate them. Indeed there are many today who know not that the dolphin even exists. They are unhappy souls and laughter is non-existent in their lives.

It is time the conceited ones realized the lack in their life that causes their conceit. It is time the arrogant ones stopped their performing and questioned the meaning of life. It is time all became creators of peace, joy, love and harmony. These things are only possible when there is happiness and laughter, and it is only possible to appreciate and value life and the meaning of it when one has undergone deprivation of it.

It is time living creations of the Creator of All regained their creative ability. It is time dolphin families increased. It is time human beings gave thanks and appreciation to the One who gave them life, to the One who created all.

I am the Light of Dolphin.

PEACOCK

 AM THE SPIRIT OF PEACOCK.

The peacock is a magnificent bird. All who see it know what I say is true. The hen's colouring is insignificant when compared to the colouring of the male. The male delights all who gaze upon him. There is a great difference in the nature of the hen and the cock. The hen is a sensitive creature. Her favourite colour is the blue of the sky. The cock knows this and to earn favour with her he will gather and collect anything that is blue. He will present them to her with a great flourish. The cock is a performer. He loves to have the centre stage. If the cock is ignored he becomes annoyed and persistently performs or acts to gain attention.

In most cases the colours of the cock's feathers range from blue to green to black. The bluer his feathers are, the more he delights in his appearance because he knows blue is the hen's favourite colour. The male is a vain creature. It is the cock's vanity that undoes him.

Long ago, when Peacock was originally created, he was a bird of great magnificence. He proudly walked the Earth and majestically flew in the air. Those who knew him greatly admired his beauty and respected him. His bearing encouraged respect. His behaviour encouraged praise. He was regarded by all as a regal creature.

One day a stranger visited the place where peacocks dwelt. That stranger was fascinated by the grandness and magnificence of Peacock. He couldn't believe a creature of such beauty and glory existed. That one was Crocodile. Back in the time of long ago, Crocodile lived happily with all creatures. He lived in the waters of Earth and walked the land but he could not fly. The flight of Peacock fascinated him. He would watch Peacock for hours taking off and landing and long to be able to do such a thing.

Peacock enjoyed Crocodile's admiration. He even began to bask in it. He had only ever been given loving respect and was quite unused to adoration. He began to preen himself and become quite vain. This greatly annoyed the hen. She became ashamed of his increasing vanity and refused to look upon him. This upset him greatly because, although he was better-looking, she was smarter. It was her smartness and cleverness that attracted him. She, when alongside him, gave him stability and encouragement. Without her he was unstable and insecure.

Crocodile knew this and began to entice the cock away from the hen. He wanted the actor to be exclusively his. The hen became annoyed and upset by her mate's neglect. When he returned from performing for Crocodile she would ignore him. That the cock could not tolerate because he was beginning to believe none could not admire him. He began to perform in front of her to show he cared. He spread and displayed wide his beautiful coloured feathers. He even began to dance to impress her but she kept her head turned and refused to gaze upon him.

In despair Peacock turned to Crocodile. That wily one invited Peacock to return to his home. Peacocks cannot swim. They are not water creatures. With his pride hurt by his loved one, the cock went to the home of Crocodile. He gazed with fear into the deep water. He flew into the branches of a tree that overhung the water, and gazed lovingly and longingly at the image of himself in the water below. In his vanity he overbalanced and fell.

Crocodile laughed in glee at his discomfort. His beauty had become lost. His feathers clung together and were heavy. The weight of them dragged him beneath the water. He was fearful and bitterly regretted leaving the safety of his home. Had it not been for a platypus, Peacock would have perished. Platypus rose from beneath the water and took the helpless bird on his back and swam with him to shore. Without even saying thank you Peacock rushed home to his mate. He received a great shock when he saw her. Where once her feathers were the same as his, they had changed colour and become less. She no longer was the beautiful creature he loved. With the pain of rejection she had become a different bird. She turned from him.

Peacock was most unhappy. He knew Crocodile was not a true friend, and his mate rejected him totally. He stood in the sun and displayed his feathers which in those days were the blue of the sky. As they began to dry, differing colours appeared, but what was most amazing to those who compassionately viewed his discomfort was the eye that was manifesting in his long feathers. All knew he would forever be watched but never trusted again. He wore the mark of vanity and distrust. He wore the evil eye.

To this day the peahen does not trust her mate. The cock is forever trying to impress her with his charms, but she knows he is easily distracted by his own vanity. The blue gifts he brings her, she rejects. No longer does she gaze at the blue sky with love. The older she grows, the greater she appeals to her mate because with age she becomes wiser. The cock forever remains immature and insecure in nature.

I tell you the story of Peacock to teach vanity and pride. The hen is a proud bird. The cock is vain. Whilever vanity and pride exist there can never be togetherness. These things are the cause of separation.

There is much separation in the lives of Australia's people today that is caused by rejection, pride and vanity. Go home, I say, and repent. When there is repentance, there is forgiveness. If the cock had repented when he returned home the hen's colours would have shone brilliantly. He did not so they became lost to each other.

To this day peacocks cannot swim. They dislike the rain and hate being wet. Their beauty is marred, they believe, by water. Beauty is within. It is a quality of the soul. Those who judge another by what they see are fools. Beauty is more than skin deep. It is not only the cock today who is proud and vain. It is not only the hen who is rejected and pained. Both cock and hen have suffered pain, rejection, vanity and pride. When these things are released from the lives of Australia's people is when the species of Peacock will regain its former splendour and regality.

I am the Spirit of Peacock.

WHITE DOVE

AM THE SPIRIT OF THE WHITE DOVE.

The dove, to many people, symbolizes peace, tranquillity and love. The dove is a bird of great symbolic significance. Dove means peace. When the birds of the air were created, it was Dove that came first. In that time of long ago all creatures had peace in their hearts, but Dove had a spirit of peace. Peace was her vibration.

Dove, wherever she presented herself, had the ability to effect peace. As time went on, whenever there was disquiet or upset, the creatures involved in the upset would invite Dove, and her mere presence effected an instant solution.

Down through the ages Dove herself has become a bickerer. It is sad but true; she provokes arguments with others. She will brook no interference in the running of her life or the lives of others, if she's allowed to run them. Dove is not content with her state of being today. She dislikes being unnatural to the true nature of herself, and because of her dislike of self, she angrily persists in provocation. Dove of today is of the vibration of provocation. In provocation she will drag from her body beautiful white feathers and cast them from her with anger and distaste. She dislikes being white. She dislikes the spirit that she herself has become.

Original Dove's feathers were brilliant, shining white. They were fluted, and glowed in the dark. Her eyes were the blue of the sky on a perfect day, and she spent much time being still, attuned to the nature of Mother Earth. Dove loved to communicate with the nature of Earth and would often be seen, with eyes closed, silently meditating, in communion with nature spirits. The spirit of silence or quietness always accompanied her because when there is peace, noise is nonexistent. Dove was a bird of reservedness. She was revered by Earth's creatures. She calmly accepted the reverence she was given with quiet reservation. She was totally unaffected by the peaceful offerings that were given to her in appreciation of, and gratitude for, the harmony and peace she created whenever and wherever she appeared. Dove was a true bringer of peace and worthy of being revered.

Reverence is a vibration that has gone missing during the passage of time. In the time of long ago, it was given to one who had purity of soul. That purity was easily recognized by the glow of light that emanated from and surrounded the Pure One. The glow came from within. It was the light or the spirit that created peace. Dove knew this and never allowed the reverence she received to affect her. She knew she was an instrument for the light to work through. She knew she was an instrument to transmit or give peace to others.

Unfortunately, as time went on, the light within Dove began to dim. Her feathers lost their brilliant glow. She began to squabble and bicker, and by doing so she lost the reverence she once received. She began to tear out her feathers in provocation, frustration and disappointment. She became vain. She needed the old reverence to feed the nature of her devolving self. She began to worship herself in her vanity and treat others with disdain. Dove today is a complete turnabout to Dove of olden time. She has forgotten she was created a spirit of peace.

The dove mirrors many people of Earth. People long to live without provocation, squabbling and bickering. They long to be respected and looked up to, they long to live in peace, but that can never be while there is ignorance of the spirit within. Whilever ignorance prevails, the soul cannot be true to itself, it cannot shine or create peace.

Man does not tear out his hair but the hair of many becomes less until it disappears altogether. Wherever there is baldness there is ignorance of spirit, and that one leads a life of turmoil. It is impossible for one with a bald head to have peace. In the time of long ago, people's hair grew with abandonment, it grew thick and long, and it grew quickly. Hair was a sign of peace. The more hair one had, the greater the soul was acknowledged and appreciated. Many today have thin, lank hair; it lacks lustre and shine, but throughout time there have never been as many bald-headed people as there are today.

I am the Spirit of Peace. It is destined that peace return to Earth. The dove of old is being reborn. This one is quietly but surely being placed in positions on Earth where her presence is most needed. By her presence in these places she is shining light of old to those who are bald. I use the word 'bald' symbolically. However, it is true that one who is bald will grow hair when the creative spirit within awakens. Peace on Earth can only be when there is peace within Man. For there to be peace within Man, Man must discover the spirit within himself, he must discover he is part of a creative spirit far greater than himself and worthy of great reverence. With this discovery, provocation, squabbling, bickering, vanity and disdain will fade from his life, and he will become a being of light, he will become a peace-bearer, he will become a dove.

As Man grows in light, the feathers of all doves will gain lustre. When all men become bearers of peace, the white dove's brilliance will be seen by all on Earth. The white dove is the incarnation of a great soul. When there is peace on Earth, the Great One will return to the heaven where it belongs. When there is peace on Earth a new star will appear in the sky. It will be the sign that the Great One's work on Earth is finished and his spirit has returned home.

The great one is the Christ Spirit. This spirit is awakening in all men. When Jesus of Nazareth was born, great light was seen in the sky from Earth. When there is peace on Earth, that same light will again be seen. Jesus of Nazareth was a christed soul. He was born with the light or the spirit of the dove. When all men are doves, great light will shine from the Christ Star to and through them and there will be peace on Earth. Man will, in time, look to the stars again, and with great reverence acknowledge the Great White Spirit, the Creator of All.

I am the Spirit of the White Dove.

ALBATROSS

AM THE SPIRIT OF ALBATROSS.

The spirit of Albatross is a spirit of kindness. Many know not this bird, but those who reflect him are bringers of joy. The albatross is himself a very noble fellow. He has simplicity of soul. By this I mean he is totally unaffected by the actions of others. To be of the vibration of simplicity, non-reaction must be present.

Albatrosses are pleasant fellows. If one needs support, encouragement or a friend, they appear. It seems they materialize from nowhere. There is a saying: 'To reject an albatross is to bring bad luck and the appearance of an albatross is a sign of good luck'.

It is not possible to ever really get close to or friendly with an albatross. This is because of his non-reaction vibration. He observes many things but never allows closeness. He always prefers casual acquaintance to kinship. This does not mean he chooses separation; he is simply at the evolutionary stage of detachment from emotionalism. When one has detachment from emotionalism, one can assess a situation with great clarity. This is the quality Albatross possesses. He is of the vibration of friendship. A true friend shows kindness and sincerity. The reason he does not allow himself to become intensely involved is, he instinctively knows, that if he allows himself to become attached he will lose his simplicity and brotherly kindness. Albatross is the friend of all men. He is the companion to those who fear, who doubt, who are lost. He is, if you like, a saviour of souls. He gives service to Man by his very presence.

Albatrosses are lone creatures yet they are rarely lonely. They have detachment from negativity. They are survivors. Before a storm an albatross will appear. He will not be seen while the storm rages, but when it is over he will appear and the sea will become calm.

To a great extent Albatross has kept pace with the hands of evolutionary time. He is friend to the dolphin and the whale. These creatures have much in common with him.

Back in the time of long ago, Albatross had attachment. It only happened once. He learnt the lesson of detachment very quickly and very well. Albatrosses are exceptionally intelligent.

Albatross had a friend. He loved this friend with all his heart and all his soul. They were true soulmates. The friend wanted Albatross to be exclusively his, to reject all others from his life, and commit himself to one friendship. To please him, Albatross did this. He became a lost, sad bird. He felt his kindness slipping from him and his sincerity fading. He actually experienced his own devolvement, and because of his intelligence he realized what would be his future.

Albatrosses, when they are human, are true humanitarians. They cannot confine themselves to one, intense relationship. If they do they become lost. They actually detach from the true vibration of themselves which is universal. This does not mean they do not mate; it means they mate with brotherly love and detachment from negativity.

Young albatrosses are born with detachment. Those who understand not the Brotherhood of Man often feel rejected by what they regard as their insensitivity. Albatrosses are most sensitive. They are sensitive to the soul, not the personality. This the little person understands not. The little person desires attachment. The evolved person desires detachment. Only through detachment from intense relationships is it possible to relate with sincerity and kindness to all.

At this point in time there is much evolving taking place within humans. Those with intelligence and depth of soul see the error of emotional attachment and they, like Albatross of old, are choosing to reject personal attachment. These are the ones who know they belong to one family, the human family. They know all men are their brothers and they cannot reject their brothers. These are the ones who today hold out their hand in friendship and sincerity and will help their mother, Earth, and their brothers evolve to become survivors, as they themselves have become.

The albatross has appeared this day because a friend was needed. With true sincerity I tell you his truth.

I am the Light of Albatross.

SEAL

 AM THE SPIRIT OF SEAL.

Seals are of the vibration of soul. They have the ability to attune to the soul of the ocean. They are of the elements water and earth. If they were solely water creatures they would not have the intelligence they possess. It is the combination of earth and water elements that allows them soul contact.

When one has attunement of soul, one is instinctively attuned to the soul of all like souls. Ocean tides move with air currents and the help of the moon. Oceans are alive. They are living water spirits that are unaware of their own spirituality. They are controlled by forces other than themselves. Oceans are subjected to great inconvenience and suffering because they are dependant on spirits or elements they do not comprehend. The waters of Earth many times are quite unpredictable. Often they are in turmoil or conflict. It is rare an ocean is still and totally at peace. If it were not for an ocean's children or its sea creatures, it would, you might say in Earth words, become insane. An ocean's creatures give it balance or sanity. Without them it is a constant victim of elemental circumstances. The elements are themselves not sane or balanced at this point in time. There is much going on unconsciously beneath the waves of oceans.

The ocean that is most subjected to upheaval and chaos is the Southern Ocean. Australia is affected by the flow of the Southern Ocean. Within that ocean live many seals. These creatures of the deep are sympathetic, loving, soul creatures. They feel the torment of their mother and they understand what she herself is incapable of understanding. They know she is pulled in all directions against her will, and in their wisdom they give their support and love. Where there are rough seas you will find seals. They stay until the seas become calm. Rarely are seals found in calm waters because it is their role to create peace and calmness. Once their job is done they are off to effect calmness or balance elsewhere. Because the ocean is forever on the move, so must be the seals. There are times when the seal must rest. He clambers ashore to think. It is only when he is ashore he has clarity of thought. When in the water he acts instinctively.

Seals are motherly creatures and protective of their young. They wallow in admiration, especially if it is their offspring being admired. They make good parents. It is because they are parents to their own mother, the ocean. The children are wiser than the mother. Baby seals love and adore their mother, and it is this love and adoration that all seals give, 'til their dying day, to the ocean.

The seals of the oceans have diminished over a very short period of time. This is due to the actions of Earth's children. If they only knew that it is seals that are saving the soul of the oceans, they would surely develop compassion. Without the seals the oceans, in a time of frenzied upheaval, will flood the land.

Seals are wise and compassionate. If you look deep into the eyes of a seal you will see this. They are soul creatures and the eyes reflect the soul.

At the beginning of time all seals were pure white. They were grand. Throughout time their whiteness has faded to grey and darker colours, but the babies, that are born white, are of the old vibration. It is becoming time all human babies were born of the vibration of the seal.

Many mothers of Earth have not yet quality of soul; consequently their children grow up and care not to nourish the soul of their mother. This is sad because if this situation persists, like the seal, human numbers will diminish. As the numbers of Earth's children diminish, Earth herself has less chance of attaining soul or spiritual awareness.

It is impossible for most humans to comprehend, at this point in time, the quality of love and devotion the seal vibrates to. It is a creature of great inner beauty. It can leap to great heights and it can dive to great depths. It has great wisdom, and seals that have had no association with Man have great humility and conservatism. Instinctively they are aware of the great responsibility they carry. Instinctively they know that, to preserve life, they must preserve their mother, the ocean.

This instinct is awakening in the children of Earth. In time they will forgive and forget their own hurt and assist their mother to do the same. When mothers of Earth attune to the soul of their mother, the soul within Earth will become calm and peaceful and the oceans of Earth will reflect her 'soul-ness'. Man and Seal will then be brothers because instinctively they will be soulmates.

I am the Light of Seal.

Koala Bear

AM THE LIGHT OF KOALA.

Any animal that lives among the branches of high trees resembles in nature Australia's Koala. If Man builds himself a home amidst trees, he is of the nature of the koala.

Koala craves fresh air. He requires more air than any other living creature and that is why he climbs and lives in high trees. The reason he has this requirement is that he has a greater lung capacity than a creature his size normally has, and the reason for this is he is an animal of darkness.

Many of Australia's native animals are nocturnal but in the long ago this was not the case. Koala lived his life scampering and romping with all Australian animals. They lived together in harmony. He loved to climb high into the trees and he would climb quickly to the height of any tree. He loved to do this because at the top of the tree there was more light. When atop his tree, he would place himself in a position where he could gaze at and admire the sun. His fur was not as thick then as it is today and the warmth of the sun would penetrate his skin and delight him. He would breathe in the crisp, fresh air and exhale loudly in his appreciation of life. His vision was extraordinary, as was his sense of smell and hearing. Whenever animals heard a downward scampering in a tree, they knew Koala had sensed something and wanted to share it with them. The people of the land had this same extraordinary sensory perception. They could send messages by thought and feel the answer.

As time went on Koala grew lazy. One day he fell out of his tree whilst asleep. He fell on his head and, as a consequence, unknowingly began to lose his extra sensitivity. His eyesight began to dim. His hearing began to fade. Where once he could smell the sweetest, juiciest leaf tips, he no longer could. He began to care less about climbing to great heights and he began to have breathing problems.

The other animals were quite concerned about him. His scampering was heard less and less. His titbits of information were scarcely conveyed. Over many generations Koala's sleeping habit grew and his activity, breathing and sun-admiring became less. His fur began to grow longer. His scampering no longer kept him warm.

He isolated himself among the trees, and it became that his presence went unnoticed by those who once revelled in his company. It was only when snoring or heavy breathing was heard they knew Koala was above in the trees. Because of his deep breathing laziness, his lungs began to expand to cope with his need for air. Originally they were ideal because of his deep breathing and exhalation.

It seems today Koala is a doomed animal. Man has polluted the air both he and Koala need. Man, like Koala, has many lung problems. Man, like Koala, cannot look at the sun. He senses not the companionship his friends crave. He hears not with quick ears. He has grown accustomed to putrid smells in the environment and accepts them as normal and natural. It is possible Koala will become an extinct animal. With each generation of koalas his senses are lessening. His instinct to mate is also lessening with time.

There is much Man can do. He can walk more, he can sit quietly and listen, he can practise inhalation and exhalation of the breath, and when he does these things, he will become an observer of his surroundings. He can touch and feel the trees, he can watch the sun rise and sit quietly and observe it as it sets. All this Man can do, and by doing so he will activate within himself his lost senses. Australia's people and her animals mirror each other. This is what Australians can do to preserve Koala from extinction.

As Man begins to raise his senses, his values of life will change. The reason Koala's mating instinct is diminishing is that he is an immoral animal. He cares not which animal he mates with. In actual fact his eyesight has become so poor, he sees not the one he mates with. In his laziness he no longer cares. His immorality has led to inbreeding and disease. In this respect he also mirrors Man. If Man is to survive, immorality must be exterminated. Without morality it is very possible, in fact most probable, that Man, like the koala who reflects him, will become extinct.

Koala today is nocturnal, or an animal of darkness. When he fell out of his tree long ago and banged his head, he began to forget the truth of his being. No longer does he know he is part of the plan of creation. Unless Man, who has consciousness, regains or remembers this truth, both Man and Koala are doomed.

However, I have the extra-sensory perception of original Koala. In the original plan of creation it was destined Man will remember!

I am the Light of Koala.

Honey Bee

AM THE SPIRIT WHICH WATCHES OVER THE HONEY BEE.
The bee is to the flowers what the sun is to Man. The bee is the creator of new life. She pollinates the flowers. She takes from the male and gives to the female. The sun creates with the rain, with the wind or the air, the spirit of the land. The Spirit of Australia is a creative one. Insects mirror the spirit of the land. Australia, like her people, knows not the spirit within.

The honeybee gathers pollen, distributes as she gathers, then carries it home to her family. The honey bee of today is far removed from the original honey bee created. That one was a majestic insect. Trees and flowers grew in profusion, and Bee spent her time visiting and communicating with all growing things. The hive the bees lived in and where they stored their honey was different to the native bees' hive of today.

Dying trees would offer themselves to the bee. While there was still life in the tree the bees would make their home. This may sound very strange today, but today we know not of the harmonious way nature had in the long ago. The bees would clear and clean old wounds. They would seal openings in the trunk of the tree. They would rid the tree of anything that sapped its last strength, and then they would hum and sing it to sleep. Trees did not undergo the slow death many of them do today. With the help of the bees, their life ended quickly. As the spirit of the tree left, there was a hollow left in the trunk of the tree. This was to be the bees' home. It was a prearranged plan between the bees and the tree before it died.

Trees grew tall in long ago time. The girth of them was immense, and many, many bees made hollow trees their home. It would be incomprehensible to the beekeeper of today to visualize the size of the ancient bee and its hive.

As time went on the bee began to diminish in size. This was because the nectar in the flowers was not as pure as in the old days. The pollen they produced had not the strength or the creative power as at the beginning of time. This greatly affected the queen of the hive. She had to lay more eggs to produce more workers to gather the ever decreasing nectar to keep the hive alive.

The size of the trees began to diminish. The spirit of the trees became smaller, hence the hollow space was smaller, and the harder the bee worked the smaller she became. She literally worked herself away.

Drones came into being. When there was purity of all, the bee was androgynous. With devolution came the drone. The golden liquid that the bees lived on was quickly devoured by the growing number of drones, and it became necessary, if the honeybee was to survive naturally, that she become attuned to the creative spirit of the land; and that is what she did. Of all God's creatures the honey bee is most attuned to the spirit of the land, of the wind, of the rain and of the sun, and because of this attunement it has survived extinction. It is the oldest living insect species.

The honey bee lives to gather nectar and pollinate Earth's flowers. Without the bee many species of living green would cease to exist. Because of the attunement they have with the nature of Earth, bees create their home within an approximate distance of another hive. In this manner all greenness is automatically preserved because all areas are catered for. The bee allows herself to be carried by the wind when returning laden to the hive. Automatically she travels upwind when leaving the hive so she may return with the help of the wind when heavily laden.

The dance of the honey bee is interesting. Bees can communicate direction to each other. They perform a dance-like movement. They dance to the north, to the east, to the west, to the south until the direction is given of where there is a new source of honey. Honey is what they live on and live for. It is their pure liquid gold. In the old days Bee had no sting. She lovingly shared her stored honey with all that enjoyed it. Bee had such a love of nature that the nature of herself was love.

As the seasons of time changed, the gentle breezes of old grew stronger, the air moved more, the gentle showers of rain turned to torrential rain, the sun beat down with a vengeance where once it had beamed glowing warmth, and Australia's spirit became a confused one. In its confusion it reflected Honey bee. That one became angry at the changes. Instinctively she knew they boded ill for Australia and herself. It became necessary she fly higher and higher to be creative. It became necessary she mate with a drone on the wing. It became necessary there be what Man calls the queen. The queen is the mother of the hive. All of the daughters see to the needs of the mother, and because of their desire to lovingly preserve her, procreation and re-creation of plant life on Mother Earth goes on.

In times of plenty bees allows the drones to survive, but when honey is scarce their numbers must go. The honey bee knows instinctively when it is time to close down the hive to the drone. The role of the drone is to mate the queen. Although the queen's needs are ever attended to, her daughters are unconsciously conscious that should she come to harm she must be quickly replaced or the unit will perish. The queen is the mother. She is the hub of the hive. When a new queen is being prepared to replace the old one she is fed a substance called royal jelly. Royal jelly is the exclusive right of the queen, and when it is time for her to mate she is released lovingly from the hive. All in the hive work as one unit. They are one with the Earth.

The Beehive is the home of the Bee family. All return home at dusk. They hum and communicate the news of the day, they tell of the day's gathering. A Beehive is a home of females. Males or drones are not tolerated lightly. The bee resented losing its androgynous state of being. In its anger it grew a spike which is known as the sting. This sting has killed many an unwary insect that visited the home of the bee. The drone exists at the discretion of the female. If he causes disharmony, he is stung to death. It is essential to the honey bee that harmony prevail. Without harmony the hive cannot survive.

Although the drone is male, it is only every second generation of drone that is capable of mating the queen. This is a consequence of the devolution of Earth and it is the reason drones are allowed to survive. Only the strongest and most virile can fly as high as the new queen after her royal jelly inauguration. Prior to the flight of the new queen, drones are given attention also. A drone lives out his life in constant anticipation of receiving loving attention and servicing the queen. It is sad but true that after the victor mates the queen, he must die.

Australia today is not the old Australia nor is the honey bee the old bee. She has become angrier and angrier at the state of nature. In fact, the nature of herself has become a real state. She lives in a constant state of agitation; she fears weather conditions will prevent not only her preservation but the preservation of her part of Earth. She buzzes angrily. Even when working she rarely hums happily as she flies among the flowers. Instinctively she senses doom and extinction. In this respect the bee mirrors Man. Man has changed the environment of Earth. He has unwittingly changed weather patterns and by doing so he has created disharmony for Earth.

There is time for Man still to reverse the situation. He must plant more things green and live amidst the green. This will create harmony in the land, and when there is harmony, all are one. The Brotherhood of Man is something worth striving for. When Man lives and works with the family of Mankind as the honeybee lives and works within and without the hive is when there will be peace on Earth and cooperation between all nations of Earth.

I am the Light of the Honey bee.

COCKATOO

 AM THE SPIRIT OF THE COCKATOO.

The vibration of Cockatoo is friendship. It is rare a cockatoo is alone. He is one of a flock. There is great power in numbers. When there is unity, there is one voice. If that voice speaks for the good of all, miracles can be created. If one voice cries alone it often is unheard or rejected.

In the time before time, flocks of cockatoos were numerous. The tops of trees could be seen decked with white. With an updraught of the breeze the white would lift from the trees in one great mass. The very movement of the birds' wings created a downdraught that rocked the branches of the massive trees that then grew. The birds would rise in one great body, and as they did they sang with joy and happiness. The cockatoo choruses created friendship and joy. Those on the ground would raise their heads in appreciation and thank the Creator of All for the creation of the cockatoo. The birds themselves sang and flew to the accompanying sound of their own flying wings. They sang praise to the One who gave them life.

Cockatoo flocks could be heard approaching long before they came into sight. The sound that preceded their arrival was the sound of harmony. All sang in unison. Each bird was an individual, but each bird was part of a group or flock. The spirit of Cockatoo is a group one. Cockatoos cannot survive alone. They must have companionship. Without friends Cockatoo is insecure. He is a lost soul.

Cockatoo of today is an insecure bird. Flocks exist still, but their numbers are small compared to the old days. They do not fly with precision or harmonious formation. They are no longer unified. Their once famous choristers screech abuse at each other instead of singing group praise.

Cockatoo of old was pure white with a yellow comb. The yellow reflected intelligence, the white his purity of soul. The black cockatoo was created after time began. Hidden beneath his black feathers are red feathers. Wherever there is red there is destruction or separation of the one spirit. The black cockatoo is a lone bird. He is not part of a flock. He has no friends. He has survived through time by cunning intelligence. The black cockatoo is a bird of darkness. He is the first bird to leave the nest in the morning and the last bird to roost at night. He is forever on the wing screeching and seeking unity with others. Whilever he screeches, he will never find acceptance.

Both black and white birds today reflect Man. Man comes in the colours of black and white. The black man cares not for the white man's friendship, and the white man cares not for true friendship of any man. The white race has become like a flock of white cockatoos: much screeching and wing flapping takes place, but there is great insecurity and disharmony. The sound of unity and one voice is unheard. The bonds of friendship the black man had with his brother have snapped, and he walks alone. He walks with regret and sadness.

The black man and the white man can come together in friendship if they choose to. Whilever separation exists between the human races, the birds of the air can never fly or sing together in harmony. Both races are part of a group soul. The black race reflects purity of soul. The white race reflects intelligence. Together the black and white races equal the vibration of the cockatoo. The two races of Man and the cockatoo are devolved creations today. When the black and the white man realize each reflects the other, they will come together in friendship, they will come together as brothers; and when they do, the Brotherhood of Man will be established on Earth.

The white man today is insensitive to the vibration of soul, and the black man comprehends not the white man's intelligence. The black man's sensitivity has been dimmed by white man's culture, and white man's technology is out of step with the spirit of Earth. Whilever there is separation of human races, the black cockatoo will replace the white in numbers.

Today, white man's intelligence is not the intelligence of soul. White man's technology will destroy him. Black man's sensitivity is not intelligent. It will destroy him. Intelligence and soul or sensitivity must go together. Whilever there is separation there is insecurity, and self-destructive tendencies. The time has come for the white man to intelligently and sensitively hold out his hand in friendship to the black man, and when he does, the black man will sensitively and intelligently respond. They will be soulmates, and together they will create for the highest good of Man and his mother the Earth.

When all men realize and individually accept they are one of a human family, great power will be invoked on Earth. There is no power technology can create greater than the power of the one voice. When there is unitedness between the children of Earth, the spirit of Earth will awaken and she will consciously transform herself into a celestial being of great light. That time is far into the future but, children of Mother Earth, it is destined Earth will be restored to her former glory. It is destined the cockatoo flocks of old return. It is destined the black cockatoo become extinct. It is destined the Brotherhood of Man precede the one human family or group soul. How do I know this? I am the Spirit of Cockatoo. I am of the vibration of friendship. Friendship is only possible when one is an intelligent soul. When one is an intelligent soul one is attuned to the one soul and one knows of the destined part one is to play in the original plan of the Creator of All.

I am the Spirit of Cockatoo.

SPIDER

 AM THE SPIRIT OF SPIDER.

The creation of Spider was done with great intention. There are many different spiders. All were created with a specific service to fulfil. There are spiders that spin webs in the open. They are air elementary. There are spiders that burrow beneath the earth. They are of the element earth. There are those which live in furnace-like conditions. They are of the vibration of the fire element. And there are those which make their home near water. These are water elemental spiders.

All were created with the intention of reflecting the elements of Earth to Earth and Earthlings. Spiders are magnetic creatures. It is their magnetism that enables them to survive. A spider with little magnetism spins a web. She forever runs around caught in her own web. The web also catches unsuspecting ones which become her prey. Spiders spin webs in all elementary places. There are other spiders with greater magnetism. They do not need a web to catch prey and survive. They attract by sheer willpower. The stronger the will, the greater the magnetism. A spider or insect with little or no will of its own is doomed when in the presence of a spider of strong will. It simply takes over or possesses the will of the other.

A spider that can survive in only one element of Earth is a weak-willed spider. A spider which can live in all elements (fire, earth, air, water) of Earth is a strong or powerfully-willed spider. Most spiders of Australia are harmless creatures. They are fearful and hide from Man. They are helpless because their will is weak, but there are some Australian spiders that are deadly. These are the ones of strong will. They can survive in most unlikely places. Their magnetism is great. They attract and mercilessly torture their prey to death. They show no remorse for any of their actions. Some of these spiders, after mating, deliberately and decisively take possession of the will of their mate and torture that one to death. The possessed one is helpless. Its will is taken. It is like a zombie that is magnetically controlled.

Back in the time of long ago there were not the spiders there are today. The spider was a creature of incredible intention. The will it was created with was a good one. It was most magnetic. Whatever Spider willed instantly manifested. He was a magician if you like. His power seemed incredible to his companions. Back in those days all needs were met for all creatures so Spider spent his time spinning magic or creating miracles. He used to dream the days away.

His friends would suggest he create a sunrise at sunset or turn night into day and so on. Many hours were spent creating with goodwill for the enjoyment and pleasure of his companions.

With the passing of time the goodwill of Spider began to lessen, and as it did he felt his magnetism slipping from him. He was losing his magical skills. He became quite distressed and insecure. He had to work to survive. He had to spin a web instead of spinning magic. He had to make his own nest, web or home by his own wit. This took much time and left him with none for daydreaming.

When Spider was of the vibration of goodwill he was powerful. It never occurred to him to possess or control the will of others. As he lost his good intentions he became selfish, and developed self-will. He also lost his magnetism and miracle magic. I say he lost his magnetism. That is not quite true. He lost the ability or the power to create with good intention. His powerful will of goodness became a will of badness.

Those who fear the spider have much to learn about themselves. They have much to learn about their own will. If one is a victim caught in the web of a spider of strong will, one has little chance of survival. The spider is the controller of those in his web. To break the web of a spider does not give one freedom. A web has many strands; each one is like a tentacle constraining the victim. The spider of deadly magnetism is elusive and clever. He is a dark-willed spirit and will never willingly release his prey.

Today on Earth there are many people with little or weak will. They are powerless. They have no control over their own lives. They are victims of their own circumstances. They cannot escape from the web of their own life's making. Unfortunately, there are others whose will is strong; they care not for the little ones. They care only for power, possession and destruction. There is no goodwill in these ones, and if allowed to persist, they will not only self-destruct, they will destroy all little ones as well.

The four elements of Earth are in disorder. While there is disorder, the will of Earth is weak. Whilever bad will is present in Earth's children, Earth is a victim of the deadly spider.

Earth's children, like many spiders of today, are out of their right element. Their will is selfish and they care not for those who are victims or crushed and broken by the power of another. When children of Earth begin to care about their brother is when the magnetism of the deadly spider will be broken. It is through the goodwill of another that the victimised ones will be freed. All who practise goodwill with a loving heart and mind can create miracles. They can move mountains, as did Spider of old, and they can awaken the will of the little ones to goodwill.

It is the will of good that breaks the will of bad. The will to live is stronger than the will to die. Light will always overcome darkness. Where there is light, there is magnetism. This magnetism is superior to the magnetism or power of darkness. Use light power, with goodwill, to benefit all.

I am the Light of Spider.

KANGAROO

AM THE LIGHT OF KANGAROO.

The spirit of Kangaroo is totally unique to Australia. It was necessary this animal be created differently because Australia is a country of vast differences. Kangaroo can travel great distances in a short period of time. Man has greatly restricted his ability to do this by building countless fences. Nevertheless, they only slow him down; they do not prevent him covering much ground.

In the time of long, long ago Kangaroo had no tail. He did not need one because he did not travel far. He had no desire to wander. He was happy and content living with nature's creations. He was friendly and amiable to all. He loved to graze beneath trees which harboured parrots of many colours. Today Kangaroo is colour-blind, but back in the time of long, long ago he not only saw the colours of parrots, he saw the colours of the rainbow all of the time. Everything he cast his eyes on glowed with colours of the rainbow. Kangaroo could see nature spirits. These ones were responsible for the growth of the trees, the flowers, the animals, and the birds. He could clairvoyantly see a red nature spirit surrounding a red parrot. He could see the nature or spirit of all things by the colours surrounding it. He lived in harmony with the colours of Australia. He loved to watch the golden sun rise, and communicate with the Spirit of the Sun. His favourite time of the month was when the moon was full and his friend's silvery glow flooded the night. The colours of today have not the glory of long, long ago. The spirit has dimmed within them, and many people, like the kangaroo of today, are colour-blind.

Most of the trees, that birds now extinct flew and built their nests in, have gone. Man has removed them. Man has changed the environment of Australia, and in his ignorance he has invoked nature spirits of a negative nature. The colours of the rainbow blend together in harmony. Many parts of Australia today rarely see a rainbow; the land itself has had its spirit dimmed or subdued.

In two hundred years Man has created devastating changes in Australia. Kangaroo today fears Man. He sees an aura of darkness surrounding him. Original Kangaroo saw original Man's aura of rainbow colours.

Back in the time of long, long ago, when Kangaroo had no tail, he was a great prankster. He was always playing tricks on his playfellows, but they were harmless, fun-loving tricks. Jackass would roar, laughing in the tree above, and Kangaroo would delight in his mirth. He could trick his friends by invoking the help of his other friends, the nature spirits. He could convince a cockatoo he was an emu, or fool an emu into believing he was a cockatoo; but, like I said, all was done in fun.

About forty thousand years ago, Kangaroo woke one morning with dimmed vision. He knew not what had happened while he slept. He was agitated and began hopping about seeking his spirit friends. Many of them were missing. He began to sense fear. It was something he'd never before experienced and he did not like it. He would stop hopping and sit on his hind legs, still, listening and looking for rainbow spirits.

Hundreds of years passed, thousands of years passed, tens of thousands of years passed. Many generations of Kangaroo lived in Australia, but slowly there came a change: Kangaroo's tail began to grow. Through the years he hopped further, seeking his colour friends. The growth of his powerful tail enabled him to make great leaping bounds, but to this day he has not located the rainbow spirits of old. He is forever on the move, covering great distances, seeking them.

Jackass often keeps him company. That one always was a wise bird, but even his laughter has lost its colour. He's proved to be a good friend throughout time, but today he laughs not with childish delight; he laughs with sarcasm and cynicism. When Kangaroo looks at his old friend, he sees him surrounded by an aura of darkness and quickly looks away, disliking what he sees.

The kangaroo today is a sad animal, he is a lonely animal. The spirit of the old days has gone from him. In this respect he mirrors Australia herself and many, many of her people, but the good news is the colours are coming back; the boys and girls of today are wearing rainbow colours. As they wear more green, the fences or boundaries in Australia will come down, the grass will grow again, the trees will grow again, and the rain will come when it is invoked by the nature spirit of the animals, of the flowers, of the trees, of the birds, of the people. The Spirit of Australia will glow with the warmth of the golden sun and the light of the silver moon, and when it does, the rainbow spirit will again manifest. Kangaroo will see nature spirits of all colours and so will the boys and girls.

This time is coming quickly. The animals, the birds, the trees, the flowers, and the people are tired of living with the colours of gloom and doom. The people long for the peace, harmony and joy of a time they sense they once knew, and they, like the kangaroo, will cover much territory in their lives to regain it.

The kangaroo is unique to Australia. Australia's people are unique to Australia, but what is most unique is Australia herself. She is awakening from darkness. She herself is beaming the colours of the rainbow spirit. It is this spirit that became dimmed by time. Nowhere else on Earth is there to be found the spirit of fun and mateship that is in Australians. Nowhere else on Earth is there the determination and persistence of the kangaroo to turn the hands of time. Time cannot be turned back. It is time the hands of time turned to the rebirth of the rainbow spirit. Fellow Australians, this is happening now. This is what is unique about Australia. The Spirit of Australia is awakening from its Dreamtime.

I am the Light of Kangaroo.

Possum

AM THE SPIRIT OF ALL POSSUMS.

When one plays possum, one plays hard to get.

The possum is a likeable creature. He closely resembles Man in that his eating habits are undesirable. All of God's creatures that walk the Earth were created to live off the Earth. Man has broken away from this natural way of being and so has Possum. Man eats highly non nutritious food today and so does Possum. Possum has become lazy in his food gathering. He prefers to live now in areas close to Man so he can live off what Man supplies. This is not good because neither Man nor Possum is eating as they were created to eat.

The possum can see with great clarity in the dark. He is a nocturnal animal. Man is changing to a nocturnal animal. Although he cannot see in the dark, he is more wakeful in hours of darkness than he is wakeful in hours of light. This is because Man has devolved to darkness.

Nocturnal means night. Unless the moon is bright, nights are dark. Possum is an animal of darkness. When the moon is full, Possum is most active. All possums are born when the moon is full. The possum's mating is instinctively attuned to enable the newly born to arrive at the time of the full moon. Man, with time, will regain the mating instinct of the possum. When the moon is full is when all creatures of the night have the most vitality. The full moon gives off the vibration of strength to creatures of the night.

People who play possum are born when the moon is full. Instinctively they are attuned to the underworld or to the unconscious world. Possums unconsciously are attracted to people who were born when the moon was full.

One can learn much from a possum if one studies him. He will sleep through the day and be active of a night. He is of many colours. Possum fur is like rabbit fur, coarse yet soft, and the healthier he is, the shinier it is.

Possums will become friendly with humans but only if humans cater to their needs. In this respect they are like humans. Humans in most cases—I say most cases because it is true—develop friendships to receive, not to give.

A possum will make his home in a hollow log, a sheltered tree, or any dark place that is secluded. He likes to be private because he is a private animal. However, he is not particular about hygiene. He will unwittingly urinate and foul his bed. Man today is of this same vibration. He cares not that he is creating his own downfall by acts of indiscretion.

The possum is subject to a virus or a disease that is similar to Man's disease of today called AIDS. This disease kills all possums. An old possum would be ten years of age.

Possums are creatures of habit. They like their own home and will keep the same home all of their life. Because of their dirty habits they create disease for themselves. They do not have a strong immune system, and if they have a cut or scratch, which they often do have, it becomes infected quickly. Possums carry ticks and other vermin. They have long claws and sharp teeth, and they scratch and bite to rid themselves of itching annoyances; hence they open themselves to infection and disease.

Not all possums know Man. There are white possums. These ones live in areas that are green. Many possums live alongside Man, but the white possum knows not Man. He lives solely on leaves and ber-ries. He lives as he was created to live. His fur is soft and luxuriously white. If he comes under Man's influence he changes his habits, and as a consequence his fur coat turns grey, then darker with each offspring until he is of the devolved possum known to Man.

Possums are not intelligent animals. They are lazy. They wander around in the darkness except when the moon is full. It is then their scampering is obvious; they are then at their most active.

Possums crave attention yet they are shy. If Man pampers them they will overcome their shyness, and even present their young to be admired. There is no greater reward you can give a possum than admiration of its young.

To play possum is not always beneficial because one is often neglected and rejected. The possum longs to be recognized and acknowledged by Man, but his shyness often prevents this. Shyness is a possum trait. If Man is shy he is often overlooked. If Man is outspoken he is often overlooked, but if Man cooperates with the vibration of the full moon, he will be seen, he will be heard, he will be listened to, and his creativity will be acknowledged.

Time all things of importance to take place at the time of the full moon. There is nothing of more importance in the life of a possum than the birth of a baby possum.

Man can learn much from the possum. Each reflects the other.

I am the Light of all Possums.

GOAT

 AM THE SPIRIT OF GOAT.

The goat is a unique animal. He is a timid, shy creature. In his original state of being he was honoured by other animals. He was honoured because of his naturalness with all.

Goat of today bears little resemblance to his forbears. In many cases his timidness has become aggression and his manners, which once were beyond reproach, leave much to be desired.

The young goat bleats and, as he grows, his bleating changes to persistent calling to the spirits of nature to come to his aid.

In the old days goats had inner vision. They could see into the dimension that is unseeable today. They could hear with the inner ear, and they listened attentively to that which was conveyed to them by ones who today humanity cannot see. Goat of today has lost his inner vision and clairaudience yet instinctively he knows there is something he has lost touch with. This makes him jumpy and quite nervous. His lost senses have not become totally retarded yet he has no control of them.

Goat will sometimes raise his head high and gaze into the distance, listening. His eyesight is good yet he sees nothing. His hearing is acute yet there is nothing to be heard. He then will baa the sound peculiar to him, and continue with what he was doing prior to his seeking for that which is beyond him.

The goat, like Man, knows there is more to life than that which he sees. It is that which is missing he yearns for yet cannot find.

Goats have many qualities that are unrecognised. Their stamina remains constant. They are surefooted and light on their feet. If they have a path to follow they will climb to the top of a mountain in double quick time, but if they have no path to follow they will quickly lose direction.

The goat that is a farmyard animal is the most lost of all goats. It is not natural for a goat to be penned or tied. The young will bleat unceasingly and the old never gains maturity. Goats must be continually led. They are unable to make their own decisions and, if forced to decide, will inevitably follow a wrong direction. It is sad but true that this is the same situation with Man today. He longs for freedom yet, when given it, knows not in which direction to go. Like the goat he can see clearly, he can hear clearly, yet the true path eludes him.

Goats can be regal or they can be most humiliated creatures. A goat overcome with humiliation is sickening to watch. This one will literally allow itself to be torn to shreds by those who should and do know otherwise. Always humiliation accompanies insecurity and doubt. Those who are lost on the pathway of life become the targets of other goats. When goats lock horns in battle they are awesome. They will fight with persistence to the bitter end. The victor slinks away in disgust at his own behaviour, and the beaten one cowers in a humiliating way. Neither victor nor loser is happy at the turn of events. The victor is irritated with himself for belittling and humiliating, and the loser despairs. Both animals long and yearn for the old days when the glowing, shining one led the way. Goats today cannot see or hear the unicorn but they know instinctively he exists, and if they can only make contact he will lead the way for them to follow.

It is possible to see and hear in other dimensions but only when one chooses to walk the path without fear. The path is there. It can easily be seen but not with the eyes and ears of Man. Man, like the goat, has lost inner sight and hearing, and with their loss he has become filled with doubt and insecurity. He has opened himself to humiliation, degradation, fear, and aloneness.

Many goats are lonely animals. In their loneliness they become smelly and unkempt. Their once timid friendliness becomes absurdity. They will nervously act in a manner that is perverse to them. They can become crotchety and bitter antagonists. Loneliness creates sadness, and the goat has become a lone creature. He cannot communicate easily with his fellows; he has lost the knack and it saddens and disquiets him. He spends much time in reflection of the past and wondering where the right path was. He seems to know there is a right path yet he still can't see it. This causes him desolation and dejection. When one is desolate, one cares no more to seek the path.

But enough of the unhappy goat. I will tell you of a new and different goat. This is the goat of today. This one is a magnificent animal. This animal is evolving quicker than any other animal on Earth. This one is leaving no stone unturned in his search for the path of life. He is climbing, climbing, climbing. He is seeking, seeking, seeking. His persistence is a joy to behold, but the really wonderful aspect of this goat is that he is regaining his lost faculties. The unicorn is presenting itself to the initiated goat and is leading him to the top of the mountain.

I have the clairvoyance and the clairaudience of the New Age goat. He is standing atop the mountain in glory. His head is held high. He has great compassion for those he sees searching for the path at the foot of the mountain and he is beckoning to them. He is calling to them to follow him. He is a regal fellow. He will never be lonely. He has the stars to guide him. He will never be aggressive or humiliate his brother. He is holding out his hand in friendship, and those below look up to him. They acknowledge him for his effort and struggle. The tears roll from his old eyes as he sees the young goats setting foot on the path he so gallantly followed long ago.

The greatest honour one can bestow on a goat is to follow in his footsteps. The greatest accolade one can sound for a goat is the cry of truth.

The truth is, there is a dimension unseen by today's Man where unseen, enlightened ones dwell. Man, like Goat, cannot find the path to it, but with continual perseverance it can be found. When Man becomes desolate and saddened enough, when he becomes lonely enough, perverted enough, degraded and humiliated enough, he will look to the mountain top and strive, with unfailing strength, to create his own path to the top. This he will do with the help of the unseen ones.

I am the Spirit of Goat.

PELICAN

AM THE LIGHT OF PELICAN.

The pelican is a bird of humility and compassion. He can fly high and he can travel great distances. He is a little wobbly at take-off, but once airborne his spirit becomes one with the spirit of the wind, and he soars and dips in time and in tune with air's up and downdraughts.

He is a most friendly chap once he gets to know you, but shyness is a real problem for him. He will shy away from any situation where there is confrontation.

Before time began, Pelican communicated with all. He was a gregarious fellow. All and sundry were his friends and companions and he talked in language peculiar to pelicans, but because all were attuned, all understood him.

He was a garbler, a waffler with words. He loved to be a communicator, but communication that was deep and meaningful was not his vibration. He was of the vibration of superficiality. He loved to socialize, but all his socializing was light, superficial and friendly.

As time went on, Pelican, like all of Earth's creatures, began to lose the true nature of himself. As darkness came into existence, Pelican's light, social chattering became tinged with the sting of criticism and gossip.

When Pelican was originally created his mouth was different to other birds. It was quite large, even for a bird. This enormity was not a problem to him. He used to take his friends on flights into the sky. He was a huge bird and could carry many. It gained him more friends and influence with the crowd. In the early days he did this to give pleasure, but with the passing of time he would gather up some unsuspecting one and fly high into the sky with the terrified one held prisoner. On landing he would release his victim, and spread rumours about the behaviour of that unsuspecting one when caught unawares.

Pelican came to be quite disliked. It became that none trusted him. Many walked in fear of him. They would hear his garbled language approaching and hide. This made Pelican sad, but unfortunately that sadness turned into maliciousness, and he became spiteful and more prone to gossip and scandal-mongering. None wanted to call him friend and all avoided him. There was one exception: Crocodile! Even today there is a strained relationship of friendship between Pelican and Crocodile. Crocodile enjoys the fall of society.

The original problem was shyness. It was Pelican's shyness that caused his downfall. He did care about his friends. He was a great observer of them all, and he had compassion and great love and acceptance of them, but they could all communicate and circulate so much easier than he.

To be one with society he believed he had to attract attention to himself to be accepted. Unfortunately, his gossip and scandalmongering did not fit the bill. His mouth began to grow bigger and bigger with each garbled word he uttered. To cover his embarrassment he watched, pried and spied on society, and backchatted even more.

Those who were once his friends, the ones he'd taken for joy flights, began to laugh about and at him. They didn't even do it behind his back, as he would have done. They laughed openly. Pelican could not confront them. He never would confront. His shyness became cowardice.

Pelican today stands alone. The social set is nearby but he is not part of it. Behind his back they refer to him as 'big mouth'. This deeply hurts and humiliates him but no longer does he shy from confrontation. Pelican, if forced to confront, will react with great quickness and viciousness.

There are many pelican people walking the Earth. They utter thoughtless, hurtful words and care not how they humiliate others. They show no compassion in the use of their gossipy tongue. If you ever have the opportunity, look into the mouth of a pelican. He has a barbed tongue. All who speak with a barbed tongue suffer the consequences of their own actions. With time they find themselves friendless, and social outcasts.

It is the pelican who can change society if he overcomes his shyness. He has observed it for aeons, and during that time he has become well aware of its pitch and downfalls. He's soared and dipped with whatever was in the air throughout his creation. If Pelican will confront society with the compassion and humility he was created with, he in his own language will, with great eloquence of speech, change it for the highest good of all.

When the children of Earth change the superficiality of society, the bill or the cost which society inflicts on the individual will shrink. This change will come about by confronting the issue, not through garbled, shy words, or words spoken with a barbed tongue. It will come about through compassion and the direct action of goodwill and service to one's fellow man.

Today's society is a group of lost souls. Humanity can and will rise above socialism. Whilever one stands alone in a crowd, one has no friendship, goodwill or service to one's fellow man. It takes but one friendly gesture to eliminate the shyness of another. Only a pelican can make that gesture. Only the man who has stood shyly alone in a crowd can turn the tide of society. It is time the tide turned. I await the new incoming tide. It always brings change.

I am the Light of Pelican.

Fox

AM THE SPIRIT OF FOX.

Those who invoke the Fox are of my vibration. I am the vibration of foxiness. Foxiness is a vibration that is within all Earthlings.

When Earth was a young planet she was of a purity unknown to Fox of today. Earth was the Garden of Eden. All things of Earth grew in abundance, all grew in harmony. Fox was of the vibration of wiliness but he was a gentle, peace-loving fellow. I refer to him as he, meaning the species of Fox. At the beginning of time there was no male and female. Animals were created of a certain vibrational nature. Fox was of the vibration of foxiness.

Many today are unaware of the existence of foxiness in themselves. They are unaware they are of the vibration of Fox. To be foxy is to be wily and cunning. At the beginning of time Fox's cunning was cleverness. His cleverness, and quickness of mind and action, were appreciated and applauded by his associates. If quick action was needed, they would turn to Fox.

Fox was a playful fellow. He loved to absorb the rays of the sun and gaze at the light of the moon, and he knew his quickness or cleverness was given to him by the One who could see all and who knew all. This one Fox walked in awe of. This one Fox looked up to. In the presence of this one Fox was humble. Fox was humble all of the time because he walked always with the presence of the One who created him.

With evolution the vibration of Fox began to devolve as did all things of Earth. It was part of the plan of creation. For there to be evolution, which is an upward spiral of spiritual energy, there had first to be devolution. With devolution came separation, and the vixen came into being.

Where initially Fox was clever, his cleverness changed to wily cunning and the vixen was of the vibration of spitefulness. There was no love between the vixen and her mate. They were attracted solely for the purpose of mating. Even the act of mating was unnatural, and because of its unnaturalness it was unsatisfactory.

Fox has no compassion for his mate. He is concerned only with his own survival. Occasionally a fox will be seen seeing to the needs of his offspring and mate, but generally Fox is a lone animal. The vixen bitterly resents this neglect. She struggles to feed and support her young alone. She is protective of her babies and will literally tear to shreds any that interfere. Fox keeps his distance and watches. He is an observer of all things. It is through observance that he has developed his cunning. His once instinctive, quick cleverness is today deceit and cunning. This is not a pleasant state of being and Fox is not a happy fellow. He spends hours contemplating his own cunning and how he can achieve more through cunning and deceit.

His mate is a lonesome creature. She is most of the time heavily burdened with young or forced to hunt to feed herself and them. The wily old fox couldn't care less. The spitefulness he provokes in his mate is not a vibration of soul. Both animals are sly and spiteful. Spitefulness exists in all who are neglected or ill-treated by their mate. The more neglected one is, the more spiteful one becomes. When there is spiteful intention combined with wily slyness, cunning and deceit, the vibration of devilry is created. If a human is referred to as a devil, it is the vibration of the fox that is being referred to. It is foxiness.

Devilry is rife in the world of today and will remain whilever there is deceit and separation. Cleverness today is at a minimum. Cunning is at its maximum. Vixens abound. To be a vixen is worse than being a devil. Devils control themselves, vixens cannot. When a vixen totally loses control she becomes a crazed female, she knows not what she does, and everything she does is done in spite. Later, when she regains her composure, she regrets, but the deed has been done and so she smoulders within, ever contemplating ways of venting spite.

I am the Light of Fox. I dislike the vibration of today's Fox. This one has no humbleness. This one knows not he was created with cleverness. This one is lost in a world of his own creation. This one will create his own destruction. By the neglect of his mate she will die. Despite all this I retain the old Fox vibration. In the old Fox there is an awakening urge to see to the needs of his mate and offspring. This urge was implanted at the time of his creation. It is destined Fox regain his cleverness before he is exterminated, by his own actions, from the face of the Earth.

Spite provokes cunning. I repeat, spite provokes cunning. Wherever there is cunning, there is deceit. Wherever there is deceit, there is spite. There is no man alive today who has not the vibration of deceit and cunning within, and there is no woman walking Earth who has not spite. This is a difficult circle to intercept. If it is to be intercepted it must be done with cleverness. It must be done tactfully, with humbleness. When the fox approaches the vixen she must show appreciation of his cleverness. That is all she need do. The fox's natural spirit is the spirit of cleverness. To reject what is natural in one is to invoke the opposite energy of one's naturalness.

When the vixen came on the scene she did not appreciate the fox's cleverness, and because of lack of appreciation he lost his God-given quality. Only by his mate appreciating his positive quality can he regain it. The same goes for the vixen. The fox must appreciate her cleverness of survival. Without her cleverness there would be no foxes.

When foxes in human form appreciate the cleverness of their own creation is when wiliness, deceit, cunning, slyness, and spite will disappear from the human animal. All in their original state were created with cleverness by the Creator of All.

I am the Light of Fox.

UNICORN

 AM THE SPIRIT OF UNICORN.

To most Earthlings I am regarded as a mythical creature. All who are of the vibration of Earth alone can never see or accept the existence of Unicorn. Nevertheless I exist, but not in the dimension of Earth. Those who have purity of soul can see into the dimension of spirit; they see me and definitely know of my existence.

The unicorn is pure white. The eyes are gentle, caring, shining blue. The body is similar to the horse of Earth except horses have not the stance or the prance of Unicorn. What really sets him apart is the silver horn in the centre of his forehead.

In the long ago, before time began, all creatures, animal and human, could see the unicorn. The majestic carriage of that one was glory to behold. He was pure white light in animal form. He shone with great magnitude, and the speed with which he moved was the speed of light. The greater one's purity of soul, the quicker Unicorn manifested himself to that one, and the greater service and goodwill one extended to others, the greater service and goodwill was extended to that one by the unicorn.

I am referring to the unicorn as an animal because it is only possible for Earthlings today to be able to visualize him as such. Purity of soul, which clairvoyance accompanies, is rare in Man and animals at this point in time. I will liken the unicorn to a great magician. His magical powers are beyond the belief of third-dimensional comprehension; that is why he is non-existent to most. Those who live in the third dimension, which is the dimension of Earth, have closed minds to truth. They block their ears to anything of a fourth-dimensional nature, and totally reject anything connected with the fifth or higher still dimensions. There are twelve dimensions of Earth. The unicorn is at home in all dimensions, but not all in those differing dimensions are at home with him.

The silver horn signifies the developed state of his being. It is placed over the third eye. It is in truth his third eye. It enables him to see, to hear, to know all that is happening in all the dimensions. He can see through time. He can move through time. He is independent of time. He has evolved beyond time so it is not a barrier to him. That is why he seems to appear and disappear, why he becomes visible then invisible. He simply moves through time as if it was not there, and it is not there when one evolves beyond the Earth vibration. There is a heaviness, a dullness, a darkness, a great mass or weight connected with the third dimension of Earth. With aspiration of the soul, one raises the vibration of oneself above the third to the fourth dimension.

There is much going on in this dimension which third-dimensional ones are ignorant of. It is very easy to lose your way here. Many lost souls dwell in the fourth dimension and, by associating with them, it is easy to become lost also. The fourth dimension is teeming with souls who know not they are creations of God. Many have left the Earth's third dimension and many are waiting to visit it. These ones come from far flung places of the Universe of One and even beyond that. None in the fourth dimension can see or know the unicorn. As one approaches the fifth dimension it is possible to catch a glimmer or the glint of him. He can appear or be in the fourth or third dimension but be invisible to most.

Wherever the light of love, goodwill and service is present the unicorn appears. He comes in meditation. He comes in dreams. He comes when one is in a state of quiet reverie. He comes when he is least expected, and he speaks with his eyes. When one looks into the eyes of Unicorn, one knows all because one becomes one with Unicorn and Unicorn knows all.

The unicorn feels the desires of humanity. He knows the pain and suffering of humanity, and he knows what humanity has inflicted on itself and the animals by living in the third dimension. The unicorn is answering the cries of help from the animals, from the people, from Earth herself. Where before he was invisible, he will become visible to many in the future.

There are many invisible-to-Earth beings which dwell in higher dimensions. All long to assist Earth and her children to rise above life in the third dimension but, because of ignorance of these ones, Earthlings fear and reject what they are ignorant of. It is the way of third-dimensionals.

It is time Earthlings became aware of their littleness, of their littleness of love, their littleness of mind, their littleness of spiritual development, of the littleness of the third dimension that binds and restricts them. Earth is but a small part of the universe. The soul that is on Earth is there for a short time only; it is part of a universal soul.

The unicorn is to the animals, the rivers, the rocks, the vegetation, the air, the sun, the moon, the stars, the people, a reminder that they are all part of one great creation. There was and still is an original plan of the creation of all. That plan contains within it the development of purity of soul. It is only by purification of the vibration of Earth that one can evolve to consciousness of higher dimensions and eventually walk through time as does the unicorn.

Unicorn comes this day to those who are ready to acknowledge higher dimensional beings. Unicorn comes in service, goodwill and love. He comes to tell you it is time you saw or heard from beings of great light. He comes to prepare you so you do not receive a shock when they make their presence known to you.

Unicorn knows all, Unicorn is all. Unicorn can be the light being which guides many on Earth. Unicorn offers his services to those who would venture into higher dimensions. Those who believe in him will surely see him. Those who believe in higher dimensional beings will surely see whatever they believe.

Higher beings always emanate and are surrounded by great light and love. If this is not present, you are meeting a fourth-dimensional being. Send it home!

When one is visited by a Shining One, one is given a message from the Creator of All. The Shining One will direct you onto your path of destiny. Knights in shining armour do not all reflect light. Look deep into the eyes whenever you seek truth and remember the eyes of Unicorn. They have great depth of soul. Unicorn will look at you direct and never turn away. His eyes tell truth.

I am the Light of Unicorn.

CROCODILE

AM THE SPIRIT OF CROCODILE.

The crocodile demands great respect. He is given respect out of fear. If he does not receive the respect he believes he is entitled to he will display great anger and rage. All are in awe of Crocodile and this he thrives on. Crocodiles are not friendly fellows. It is not friendship they seek. It is respect. They are wily creatures. They will manoeuvre others into situations they have no control over and delight in their discomfort. A crocodile will never give assistance for the good of another. His only interest is demanding their respect.

Crocodile was not always as contemptuous of others' creation. In the beginning he was greatly respected. He was a great athlete. He could cover ground with great speed, and equally speed through the water. He was a two-dimensional creation. Most animals, at the beginning of time, were created of one vibration. Crocodile was two. He was two-sided.

He never was a great socialiser at any point in time, but his presence was always noted, loitering and watching. He wanted to be part of all that was, yet he didn't. To others his approach seemed quite offhand. It was too casual. He never complied with any order. He never quite knew the true vibration of himself. He never knew who he was.

Those who were acquainted with him accepted and respected his dual nature. He was always greeted cordially and included. He wanted to join in and participate yet he chose to set himself apart.

Crocodile could never be relied or depended on even when he was first created. Whatever was agreed to, he would do the opposite. He was a contradictory, disagreeable creature. He was what is today called two-faced or double-sided.

He genuinely was a confused, two-dimensional creature. When on land his thoughts would guide him. When in the water he was sensitive, and instinct guided him. He would act according to where he was. While his thoughts were of a happy, positive nature, instinctively he felt happy and positive. Crocodile himself became a victim of his own circumstances. It was this victimisation which led to his downfall and loss of respect.

Today there are many of Earth's children who are of the Crocodile spirit. They tease, torment, and provoke others into situations not for their highest good. They enjoy undermining another's confidence, are remorseless and casual in their relationships.

A crocodile's behaviour is never mannerly, considerate or consistent. This is because of his dual nature. He is torn in two directions.

Crocodiles rarely regret taken actions. Many of their actions are taken impulsively or unwisely. They live totally without fear yet invoke fear in, and demand respect from, all who know them. The only time Crocodile regrets an action is when it backfires on him. He revels in the backfiring of his actions on others. Crocodiles, when they are self-defeated, will cry copious tears of regret. These tears are like giant waterfalls which can be turned on and off at will.

Unbeknown to Crocodile is the fact that the respect he seeks is self-respect. There can never be self-respect while one is untrue to the true vibration of oneself. It is possible, at this point in time, to integrate the duality of the nature of oneself. It is by instinctively knowing that one learns to do this. One learns from past mistakes and Crocodile tears of rage and regret.

With age comes wisdom, and with wisdom comes evolvement beyond duality. This is often referred to as mastering oneself. One earns one's own respect by mastering oneself. These ones never demand the respect of others. They understand duality and disrespectfulness and are detached from and above such things. It is these ones who are given respect. They are given it because instinctively others know they have earned it.

I am the Spirit of Crocodile.

SERPENT

I AM THE SPIRIT OF SERPENT.

I come to you in peace. Back in the time of long ago, Serpent was created of the vibration of truth. That one vibrated to truth. Serpent was green. He lived in the trees. Although he was of the colour green, the green reflected all colours. Wherever Serpent went or whoever he visited, he reflected the colour vibration of wherever he was or whoever he was with, and so he became known to all as the Rainbow Serpent.

All creatures of Earth in that long ago time could see colours much brighter than can be seen today. Those who had greater development of clairvoyance could see Serpent in brighter colours. They could see him in his true colours, but they did not know the colours they saw reflected the truth of their own being.

Serpent had great knowledge and he longed to share that knowledge with his fellows. He had great knowledge but he did not have wisdom. Wisdom comes from living and experiencing the vibration of Earth. In his limited wisdom he encouraged all to seek the knowledge he was created with. As every creature was created of a different vibration it was impossible for them to equal the vibration of Serpent. That one was a persistent creature. He longed to give those he knew and loved his truth. What he did not know was that if they changed or attempted to change their natural state of being, the idyllic life situation they lived in would change also.

Serpent loved the truth, and his desire was so great to share it he literally began to force his knowledge onto his friends. At first they tolerated his behaviour. He was not satisfied with toleration; he wanted them to seek and long for truth as he did, and so his persistence intensified. It wasn't too long before he found himself being dodged and avoided. This upset him because he did in all truth want to help.

He began to stay in the trees more and visit less those on the ground. Because he saw fewer creatures he reflected fewer colours, and because he reflected fewer colours he began to lose his knowledge. Serpent did not have the wisdom to know that truth could only be gained by living with and reflecting one's natural born vibration to others, and their reflecting to him.

The more he separated himself, the slimier green he became. When he moved he would slither and slide instead of his usual gyrating method of standing with head erect and manoeuvring himself with great speed by the manipulation of his powerful rear end. Serpent did not like what was happening to him and he began to dislike himself. He learnt to his own horror he was becoming snakier.

Those who knew him compassionately observed his downfall. Where before they had tolerated his pushiness they could no longer do so, so they rejected him altogether. Serpent set out to teach Earth's creatures a lesson. He was determined they would gain truth whether they liked it or not, and he began to spend time devising a plan to trick them into seeking truth.

Rainbow Serpent's disappearance upset the balance of the nature of all things. No longer could creatures observe themselves through him, and they became confused and confounded and began to forget their own vibration or nature. Serpent watched this happening with glee. He knew eventually they would cry out for the truth of themselves.

When one is lost, time moves slowly. One day Serpent slithered to the ground. His beautiful green had changed to slimy green, and that slimy green was in the process of changing to slithery brown and even satanic black. He had grown very dark, and the colours he reflected were the dark colours of confusion, confoundedness, and ignorance.

The lost ones gazed at Serpent in wonder, then horror. They did not like what he had become, but they did not know that the colours he reflected were what they themselves had become. All had become disillusioned, lost creatures. They had lost the truth of the spiritual essence or nature of themselves.

Serpent was delighted by what he saw. He did not realize, however, that the dim, dark colours he saw in others reflected himself. Darkness or dark colours were coming into existence. The darker the colours the creatures of Earth reflected, the more lost they'd become to the truth of their own being.

Today the snake is many shades of darkness. The only time he rears his head is when he viciously and venomously strikes at another. The truth he lovingly wanted to share in the long ago is lost to him. He hides from all in shame. Deep within his soul he knows he was responsible for the fading of the colours of the rainbow. He knows he reversed the vibration of the spirit of all things.

It is time the Rainbow Spirit reared its head. It is time children of Earth recognized in others the negativity and positivity of themselves. There are many alive on Earth today who are snakes and should hang their heads in shame. It is quickly coming time for green to be worn. The snake sheds his skin and so can Earth's children. It is time truth reared its head. It is time all vibrated to the true nature of themselves. It is time confusion, confoundedness and ignorance became truth. The snake instinctively knows this, and with each shedding of his skin in the years ahead he will regain his former self, but there will be a difference. Through experience and time he will have grown wise. He will have discovered wisdom comes with transformation and change. In his greenness he never knew that. The Rainbow Serpent of the future will be iridescent green and the colours he reflects will be iridescent colours. When there is wisdom there is iridescence of colour.

If you are of the vibration of the snake, seek the truth of your own being. Seek with persistence and determination and the Rainbow Spirit of old will find a way to reflect truth to you. Each being that attains truth enables Serpent to become wiser. In his wisdom he no longer inflicts or forces his views on others. He knows, when the student is ready, the teacher will appear.

I am the Spirit of Serpent.

EMU

I AM THE SPIRIT OF EMU.

The emu is of the vibration of discretion. Emu today is most indiscreet and because of his indiscretion he is a rejected bird.

In the time before time all creatures of Earth were true to the vibration of which they were created. All creatures lived in peace and harmony. The birds of the air, the animals of the land, the creatures of the waters of Earth lived as one family. They communicated, they laughed, they sang, and they revelled in the joy of being alive. They had appreciation of life. All knew they were creations of the Great White Spirit, and in the manner of their creation they thanked and praised the Creator.

In that time of long ago there was no night. There was no darkness. Earth turned on her axis and as she turned she faced another sun. The universe was young then. During its evolution many stars have come and gone. Some have self-destructed, others became wanderers. All in the universe was, and still is, in constant motion. It is this motion that activates life on Earth and in the heavens.

Because there was peace and harmony on Earth, this was also so in the heavens because each reflects the other. The stars in the sky twinkled and shone light to each other. Many cheeky ones were known to wink. The sun shone brightly and the moon did not exist. The moon did not come into being until time began. When time began, separation began. When Earth experienced separation, the moon came into existence. It is a long story that I will not dwell on now.

The second sun, which I referred to, left the Universe of One to enable devolution. When all in the Universe of One evolve to light it will return, and again there will be no night or darkness on Earth.

Emu is of the vibration of the second sun. The second sun was most discreet. It withdrew from the Universe of One's motion when indiscretion came into being.

All stars in all universes emit light. They emit energy. This energy is received by other stars. Each needs the light of another to operate or exist. The stars in the sky can be likened to the children of Earth. The stars belong to a celestial family. Human beings belong to a human family.

When Earth turned to the second sun, the rays of that one shone discretion to Earth. All on Earth were discreet. They thanked the sun for the service she gave. There was one, however, who rejected the discreet one. That one adamantly refused to acknowledge discretion. That one was Emu.

The sun was distressed. She knew Emu was created of her vibration and she tried with determination to beam him light. She was rejected.

Emu in those days was quite a small bird when compared to his size today. He was not a terribly friendly fellow. He had a quick eye and beak. He missed nothing. His fellow creatures admired his long legs and splendid feather arrangement, but he cared not for social chitchat. Emu could fly in the time of long ago. Throughout time he has lost this ability and ruffled many feathers. Today Emu's behaviour could be categorized as stickybeaking. He would poke his nose into the business of others. He made it his business to inspect and investigate things which others would not concern themselves with because they were not of that vibration. This quite upset those of unlike vibration and he found himself rejected. Rejection was something he had no comprehension of. It intrigued him so he began to investigate it. The more inquisitive or stickybeaking he became, the more he was rejected.

He began to grow in size. He became known as a busy body because his body was busy changing. He became quite upset by this change. He was intelligent enough to realize the creation of himself was changing. He did not realize, however, that he himself was responsible for the change.

The second sun tried unceasingly to beam him light, but that one he chose not to look at. He grew so heavy his wings could not bear him off the ground. Without use, they began to wither in size. Emu became quite vicious towards his companions, and resented all vibrations of the Creator. He was left to walk alone. He was left to learn. This he does.

The emu is a lone bird. He is most indiscreet. His behaviour and actions leave much to be desired. He cares not how he offends others. He walks disdainfully but gallantly. He is a proud bird. It was his pride that created his downfall. Emu would like to have been created a peacock. His indiscretion doesn't, and never did, endear him to others. The only one who cared truly about him was the second sun, and that one shines not light on Earth today.

Emu is reaching the stage in his evolution when he has had enough of rejection and indiscretion. Throughout time, on the quiet, he has been observing humans. He has observed many indiscreet acts and been appalled by them. He himself has been a victim of indiscretion many times. The hands of time have turned, and if you make it your business to observe or stickybeak at the emu, you will see him lift his head high and gaze at the sun. He does this in a manner of regretfulness. He receives not, from the rays of Earth's only sun, that which he now longs to receive.

Discretion is non-existent in many who have long legs. They have ruffled many a one's feathers. These ones do not travel by plane. They choose not to fly. These ones have suffered from rejection of others. They have learned discretion is the greatest part of valour, that stickybeaks never prosper, and the only thing gained is loneliness.

The male emu today must rear and tend to his young. The female discreetly allows him to do so. He would like to be androgynous, as he was before time began. He regrets past indiscretions and longs to be the true vibration of himself.

There is much activity occurring in the heavens. The celestial ones are constantly moving and changing position. When it is time, the second sun will reappear, and when she does, Emu will race with admiration and respect to receive the rays she will lovingly beam to him. His wings will grow, his size will decrease, and he will fly like he never flew before. He longs and waits for that day. In the meantime the sun, Earth and Earthlings know, does its best to shine energy to all on Earth to enable them to vibrate to the true creative nature of themselves.

I am the Light of Emu.

GREEN FROG

I AM THE LIGHT OF GREEN FROG.

Wherever there is greenness, there is peace. Frogs are the most misunderstood of all God's creations. To be a frog is to be a servant. Frog labours long and hard, but his labour is a labour of love.

Frog begins her life as a tadpole. She happily swims and feels her way in waters in various places. The frog is not fussy where she lays her eggs. She will lay in puddles or in rivers, but wherever there is water you will find the green frog.

In her young life as a tadpole she instinctively survives. The water she hatches in is her home and her source of survival. Many drop into Frog's home and never leave. You might say they stay for dinner. The tadpole sees not; it is blind. This fact is unknown to most humans. The tadpole is trusting. She will go in whatever direction the water flows. This she does willingly. She trusts in nature. The tadpole is of the vibration of trust. She has trust in her own ability to survive. Tadpoles can and will survive in the most unlikely places. They are the survivors of Earth.

Tadpole remains a tadpole for as long as it takes her to trust completely in the nature of herself. Some tadpoles turn into frogs very quickly; others live but short lives and remain as they were born. Nature is a wonderful creation. If humans understood the nature of themselves and their mother, Earth, they would create everything green. Green is the colour of peace, of harmony. Without green there is disharmony and war. Trees and vegetation are to Mother Earth what air is to humans. They are her life. Without the trees, Earth cannot survive. Without Earth, Man cannot survive.

Frog is the quickest evolving creature alive. She trusts she will survive and she does. To witness the transformation of a tadpole into a frog is glory. Some transform quicker than others. The transformation is complete when the eyes open and the frog leaps, with sight, from the water. Many mature frogs gather to welcome the young frog into her new life. Whenever you hear a chorus of frogs you will know an initiation is taking place.

There are frogs of many colours. A frog can transform the colour of herself to suit her environment. Frogs other than green generally are loners. Their survival rate is low. Green frogs are great survivors; they are communal living creatures and they live together in peace. All guard and guide the young. A most important part of the upbringing is how to remain green. The green frog loves being green. She has remained green throughout time because she gives service to nature. She is a nature spirit that is visible to humans.

Frog watches and waits. Whenever she sees an opportunity to give service, she appears. She can communicate with all living creatures. It is they who can't always communicate with her. A frog always blinks when she has accomplished something to her own satisfaction. You might say she gives herself a pat on the back by a blink.

In the olden days many in need of a friend found a frog on their doorstep. Her greenness calmed their soul. Frog will still appear if she can give service; however, today she is wary. She has been mistreated by Man and by nature throughout time.

Those who reject the green frog reject transformation. They do not want change in their lives. Frog loves to see others develop and grow into a state of higher evolution. She knows one has vision with initiation, and vision enables one to view life with greater perception.

If a green frog crosses your path, say "Hello, friend" and know she comes to tell you it is time you changed the nature of yourself. She comes in peace, she comes to give you a service. She is a peacemaker.

Unfortunately there is one green frog out of step with her species. Her family accept her, trusting one day her natural transforming vibration will effect change in her. This one is green, not with peace but with envy. If a slimy, wet frog visits, recognize you are being envious and transform that envy vibration into peace.

The green frog is soft, velvet green. She has revealed herself to many throughout time by the sound she emits. This sound is but a croak when compared to the frog choruses of old. Her peace song has become quite repetitive and boring and many block their ears to it. She is a survivor and whilever she survives she will croak peace and remain green.

For Earth to survive she must have greenness. The frog, being of the nature of her mother the Earth will, to her last gasp of air, croak peace.

I am the Light of Green Frog.

Wombat

AM THE SPIRIT OF WOMBAT.

Did you know that when you say the word 'wombat' you invoke me? Even if you think the word 'wombat', you invoke me. The wombat is a wily fellow. He can outwit a crocodile, but let's not go into that yet. I am here to tell you about Australia's Wombat.

This one, in his original design, was a larger animal than he is today. Wombats are shy fellows. They like to sleep in the day and roam about during the night. They blunder along without a thought for their own welfare. They are stubborn fellows. The females are extra stubborn. Wombats mate for life. Because of their stubborn nature there is disharmony in their family relationships. You will often see a wombat bearing scars. These have been received from its mate for non-cooperation.

Wombats are placid until they are provoked. The mate of a wombat constantly provokes the other until it reacts in exasperation. Rarely do you see wombat mates together. In fact it's rare you will see Wombat. It is only when he becomes angry he goes on his blundering walkabout. He will walk into trees, into rocks, into anything in his pathway. He simply has to walk to get away from his provoking mate. Wombat longs for peace but whilever he remains mated he cannot have it.

Wombat of today reflects Man. There is much anger in the heart of Australia's people. They are stubborn, proud people. Wombats also are proud, especially of their young. The anger Australians feel towards their mates began long, long ago when Wombat was a huge animal.

Ancient people sometimes confused Wombat with the bunyip. They looked nothing alike. The only resemblance they bore to each other was the light that shone from them in the dark. Wombat was most intelligent. He, like Bunyip, could attune to the essence or 'life-force' of all of Australia's animals. Wombat was not always nocturnal. He would roam at his pleasure through the land and he would roam great distances. Always he was a roamer. He would simply roll, or so it seemed. He would roll along, enjoying being attuned with all.

One day he noticed on the horizon a great light. He could associate well with the sun, the moon, the stars. They were his family. He began to roll or blunder quickly towards the great light, excited at the prospect of a new celestial friend. The closer he came, the hotter it became. Because of his persistent nature, he continued to blunder towards what he discovered was a raging bushfire. He had never experienced a bushfire and wanted to make it his friend; he was friendly with all light beings. The fire devoured him. The story of Wombat is a sad one. It is the story of stubbornness or persistence when wrongly directed.

When our hero perished, the light within all wombats went out. Where once there had been honourable mateship the mates began to bicker. The children or young wombats mimicked their elders, and so Wombat of today came into existence. Where the wombat once rolled and roamed along freely enjoying life, today he blunders into unseen obstacles.

With each generation of wombats they began to diminish in size. Because of their blundering habit they did not roam the great distances they did in the old days. Once a wombat would travel far, seeking the one he would mate for life. Today the wombat does not wander far from his home. His eyesight is not good. He has blundered into so many obstacles his vision has become dimmed. He mates with the first wombat that crosses his path. Often it is his brother or sister so there has been much inbreeding of the wombat. Breeding within one's family is not good. The offspring are often impaired and weaker than the parents. Many young die and, as each century passes, it is noticeable that the size of the wombat is shrinking.

Wombats of today are lovable creatures but only when their mate is absent, and this is so with Australia's people. The mate restricts the natural nature of its mate. This is a sad state for all to be in because one is forever in the crossfire. Yet, like Wombat of old, all persist in walking into the firing line or blundering into the obstacle.

Whilever both persist with stubbornness and pride, nothing can be done, there can be no change. The female wombat longs to have the companionship of her mate, and he longs for the old days when she freely gave herself to him. Whilever they persist in provoking each other, it can never be. Provocation must cease. Provocation is Crocodile energy. The crocodile snaps its jaws and swallows its prey.

I said at the beginning, Wombat is wilier than Crocodile. This is because, at this point in time, he is able to realize the error of his ways. As Man ceases to provoke his mate, wombats will cease their blundering. As Man learns cooperation and exercises it, instead of blundering along alone, he will have a mate who is loyal, and together they will avoid the obstacles of life. In fact, the obstacles will become non-existent.

It has taken untold years for Man and Wombat to devolve to their present state of being, but the stars and the celestial beings who befriended wombats are still their friends. Man and animal look rarely to the stars for friendship today. Light from the stars is flooding the Earth, and as it does, both Man and animal are awakening to the true nature of themselves.

This is all I wish to say about wombats.

I am the Spirit of Wombats.

TOAD

 AM THE LIGHT OF TOAD.

Toads mirror men of today. When time began, toads began. Original Toad was a creature of complacency and diplomacy. Within every living creature there is the essence of divinity. There are some creatures that live in total ignorance of divinity. Toad is one of these creatures. He is a creature of contrariness.

To be a toad is to be ignorant of creativity. To be a toad is to show disrespect to others. To be a toad is to be a malingerer. To be a toad is to be uncreative in the interests of others and creative in the interest of self.

Toadyism creates disharmony. The toad is a creature that destroys. The toad is venomous. When there is venomousness, there is poison, there is death. Toad can be recognized by his ugliness. He is an ugly, venomous creature. He is malicious and unworthy of living and life. This one was created to reflect devolution of soul. This one devours those who would live with complacent diplomacy.

Original Toad was a peaceful enough fellow. He moved with an aura of sneakiness. All knew Toad was mischief, but always he covered his tracks with great diplomacy. He never offered assistance to others. He was complacent when it came to a friend in need. He would see to his own needs in a quiet, unobtrusive manner. He was a toad.

He was accepted for his toadyism. Whilever there was acceptance he created in the interest of himself. He was a mischief-maker. Always, when there is self-interest only, mischief is created. Others were askance at many of Toad's actions. They allowed him to mistreat and misuse their talents. There is a big difference between allowing and accepting. In the beginning of time, Toad was accepted; today, he is allowed.

Throughout time his sneakiness has developed into such abnormality that he has become his own executioner. To self-preserve, Toad must multiply, and this he also does with complacency and diplomacy. Toads care not for others. They will create toads or toadyism in the most unlikely places. To be a toad is to self-destruct.

Are you a toad? Are you sneaky? Are you self-indulgent? There is an old saying: 'Once a toad, always a toad'. That saying in itself reflects Toad. He can change himself. He is a master of disguise. He can puff himself up. He can change colour. He will lie and cheat. Toads believe they are invincible. That is their downfall. Toads are not protected by the divine. They meet death ingloriously.

I tell you of the toad because I am the vibration of Toad. I dislike myself. Always a toad or mischief-maker can be recognized by their self-defeating attitude. They will run themselves down. At this point in time it is possible for toads to eliminate self-destruction. Whilever one is of the vibration of self there is self-destruction. There is ignorance of self. The spirit within creates not for the good of all.

If the toad chooses to change himself he can do it with great expertise, complacency and diplomacy, as he does all things. Toads choose always in their own best interest. A toad will only change if change benefits him.

He was created to reflect negativity. If there was no negativity, the spirit of mischief and destruction could not be recognized. It would go unnoticed and be accepted as in the old days. We are not living in the old days. We are living now. Whilever we remain complacent towards a toad, he will diplomatically destroy with his poison. Whilever we allow toadyism, it will continue. It is time it ceased. Toads are cowards. If they are caught out they will literally turn themselves inside out.

If you are a toad this is what you must do. On the outside of a toad is negativity. Within is positivity. A toad positively dislikes what he is without. Whilever he accepts his own toadyism, he will never allow himself to turn inside out. He is working against himself instead of for himself. He is a self-defeatist. This he knows not. He is a toad.

As Man exterminates his own inner toadyism the toad will be exterminated from the Earth. Toads mirror Man.

I am the Light of Toad.

Platypus

I AM THE LIGHT OF PLATYPUS.

Platypus is a retiring soul. He is of the vibration of gentleness. When one is of the nature of gentleness, one is easily hurt. When one's spirit has been hurt and abused, one retires from the life that gave them hurt.

In the beginning, when all was new, Platypus was an effervescent creature. He bubbled with joy and contentment. He never was a great wanderer but he liked to stray a little. He was a homebody really. There was always a visitor popping in. He was a good listener to all of his companions.

Platypus loved company. His shyness and gentleness endeared him to others. If he could give service to another he willingly did so, and expected nothing in return. He loved swimming. He excelled at deep diving. He could leap from a riverbank with great stamina and speed. He would give diving and swimming lessons to any who enjoyed the water. Platypus was a water spirit at heart. Although he frequented the land, he was more at home in the water.

All creatures had highly developed senses before time began. Platypus's gentle nature was much gentler then than it is today. When there is gentleness there is great sensitivity. One is attuned to all things. If a fellow creature was happy, Platypus was happy. If he heard song, he felt like singing. Whatever were the vibrations of others, Platypus's gentle nature absorbed or attuned to them. This was a delightful state of being, while all lived a life of peace and harmony. It was destined, in the plan of creation, that that idyllic existence be phased out to enable all spirit or creations of the Creator of All to evolve.

Platypus felt stress more than any other living creature. He felt the stress of all. He felt the pain of all. To escape from this pain he became a recluse. He cut himself off from his companions and retired. He did this in an effort to regain the peace he knew in the old days.

One can never run away from problems, and this Platypus discovered. In his reclusion he suffered greater pain and stress. He had none he could share problems with, and those who knew him left him to his own devices, believing that was his desire.

If you are fortunate enough to witness a platypus you will be amazed at his antics. He always does the unpredictable. He enjoys his own eccentricity. He never interferes in the lives of others, and will brook no interference from others in his own life. The platypus and his mate can be likened to the proverbial Darby and Joan. Life goes on around them, but they prefer to live their own lives.

The eccentricity of Platypus is most interesting if studied. He is a genius in the eyes of others. In his own eyes he is worthless. His sensitivity, when it comes to others, is truly amazing, yet he is not sensitive to his own sensitivity. He opens his senses to others, closes them to himself. He gives service to others, none to himself. Whilever his gentle soul is unaware of its true state of being, his eccentricity overcomes him. He continually defeats his own purpose.

When one is a recluse, others know not their needs, others have not the sensitivity of Platypus. Because others sense not his needs Platypus believes they care not, and he feels pain. He feels neglected and unloved.

Platypus is deeply loved by those who know his gentleness. These ones understand his eccentricity and they lightly tread water when in his presence. They know he feels and is sensitive to all, and they endeavour to free him from the hurt of others. This has not until now been possible because he has been held in the grip of time. Time is loosening its grasp on Platypus. He has suffered enough. He was created of the vibration of martyrdom. All martyrs are gentle souls. His eccentricity is becoming enlightenment. He understands now his own gentle sensitivity. Give him a little more time and he will be seen in public as in the old days. He will be teaching and instructing all who desire to swim through life without pain and stress. There is none more qualified than Platypus to do this.

There are many humans of the vibration of Platypus. Their gentle vibration has absorbed as much insensitivity as it can bear. These ones have swum against the tide or floated through life in the most unpredictable manner until now. Time is changing. The hands of time are now turning with great speed. Platypus must sink or swim. Those who swim are the teachers of tomorrow.

I am the Light of Platypus.

GOANNA

 AM THE LIGHT OF GOANNA.

The goanna is to the insect what Man is to the goanna. All insects fear the goanna. All goannas fear Man. Goannas are private creatures yet they are most inquisitive. Goannas are investigators. They are the detectives of the area. There is nothing a goanna is unaware of in his territory.

A goanna will never go beyond the boundary of his abode. His abode, however, may be quite extensive. He is protective of what he believes is his.

Goannas grow in height according to their evolution of soul. Most of them today are soulless creatures, but in isolated areas untrodden by Man the large goanna of old still exists. This one stands as tall as Man himself and Man could learn much from him. The prime of those who live close to humans has faded. The more association they have with Man, the greater the decline in their size. Through association with Man they devolve. This is sad because these two have much in common they could share.

At the time when all began, Goanna was a gregarious fellow. He was often heard to laugh out loud. He had a genuine interest in the nature of all his friends. He loved and appreciated each individual for their particular individuality. The soul quality or nature of each of them fascinated him; it was the creative spirit within them which most interested him. He greatly respected the Creator of All and had tremendous admiration for the creativity of the great one. It was this creativity which fascinated him.

Goanna knew he was created of the vibration of inquisitiveness, and he was happy and content with himself. He expressed his interest in others most sincerely and with kindness. He understood animals could not fly, some birds could not swim, and many water creatures could not survive out of the water. He visited them wherever they were, and discussed nature and the wonder of it.

While Goanna questioned, he gave assistance wherever he could. He performed somersaults for the young to amuse them, and told jokes. His jokes were always in good taste. They were about himself, and creation, and the creation of Earth's creatures.

He was welcomed wherever he visited, and many a tale was told. Goanna had great strength and stamina. When in a hurry he appeared to fly along the ground. His quick action reflected his quick mind and wit. He was a witty fellow.

We know now of the Creator's plan of evolution. We know now devolution had to come first. Man himself creates obsolescence. Goanna was the first creature to recognize devolution of spirit. To say he was distressed is an understatement. He was horrified and disgusted that one he so greatly admired and respected, the Creator of All, would create such torment, such suffering, such change with deliberate intention, and he turned his back on the One who created him. By this very action he himself began creating the devolution of his own soul. He began to shrink in size. His stamina began to fade. His strength began to fail. His wittiness began to disappear and he began to wither. Then time began. The more time passed, the more withered Goanna became. He investigated the creative spirit in others less, his heart was breaking to see living creations he had great appreciation of devolving before his eyes. Goanna closed his eyes to what was happening all around him.

Goannas live to a great age. In olden time their life span was greater than it is today. The spirit of inquisitiveness is still programmed into a goanna. His territory is smaller than in olden times. His wittiness is today reflected in his quick movement of beak and tongue but he says nothing. He has nothing to say. He lost that ability also through time. Many turn away from Goanna in fear; they say he is ugly and repellent. He is a Godforsaken creature. He is a withered, lost, old soul. He is a hermit and lives alone. The goanna species will become extinct if they persist in creating their own devolution.

The goanna mirrors Man. There are many who have forsaken the One who created them. There are many who use their wits against themselves. They are sharp of tongue, inquisitive in nature, but their inquisitiveness is vindictive. Jokes they tell are slanderous. They care not that souls of differing vibrations are struggling to survive in a devolved world.

Goanna is a recluse with a difference. He shamelessly worships the moon. The moon merely reflects the sun. The sun is the symbol of the Creator. The moon is the Creator's shadow. Goanna is a creature of darkness. He is obstinate and persistent in his rejection of the Creator. Through his own actions he will exterminate himself. The creative spirit is the life spirit. To reject the Creator is to reject life.

It is time human goannas knew this. If Man desires to exist on Earth he must investigate, with great inquisitiveness, his own creative ability and the creativity of the One that created him. It is the creative spirit in Man that will awaken the living creativity in the goanna and Mother Earth herself. Without inquisitiveness one will never detect the truth.

Withering comes to many in old age. Goanna is one of Earth's oldest creatures. Withering is a creation of darkness. It is a creation of time. When there was no time there was no withering. With the time it takes to blink an eye, Goanna and humans can cut through time. Time is a creation of devolved souls.

It is time evolution of soul began. It is time withering and old age ceased. It is time all recognized they are the creators of their own evolution. It is time the Creator of All was recognized. It is time all became one with the Creator of All. It is time inquisitiveness became detection. It is time that time quickened into eternity.

I am the Light of Goanna.

BUTTERFLY

 AM THE LIGHT OF BUTTERFLY.

The creation of Butterfly was pure genius. She is a creature of high evolvement. All who are of the Butterfly vibration walk with God. They walk with goodwill in their heart and the desire to give service to their fellows.

Before time began there were myriads of coloured butterflies on Earth. Their colours were of brilliant hues interlaced with silver and gold. The golden butterfly is non-existent today, but when original Man inhabited Earth he was of the vibration of the golden butterfly. That one had a wing span that measured the length of a man's arm. She fluttered among the coloured flowers that bloomed with profusion, and gently landed on petals beginning to open and kissed them open with her touch. The touch of the golden one enhanced the beauty and perfume of the new bloom.

The golden butterfly, by her touch, awoke the living spirit in the flowers. When spirit is alive or awake it is most creative, hence the flowering shrubs and trees bloomed with prolific magnificence. Wherever the Golden One flew, or whatever that one touched, became enhanced by her presence. The touch of the golden butterfly was magic. It gave enlightenment. It created the desire within living things to create beauty.

The Golden One was always accompanied by a variety of smaller coloured butterflies. The Golden One can be likened to royalty, and her company to protectors of royalty. Although the royal guard surrounded and seemingly protected her from harm, they kept their distance and never interfered with her visits or flight. The Golden One flew alone. She had no mate. She was a creature of perfection. Only she could fly through time. When she chose, she would disappear from the Earth or third dimension. The royal guard would then rest, knowing she would appear again exactly where she had disappeared.

In the old days the colours on Earth were more brilliant and varied than they are today. There was effervescence of light. That light illuminated all it touched. As the Golden One flew through the light it became living spirit. That spirit pervaded Earth. Man today cannot remotely imagine the glory of Earth when she was a young planet.

With the coming of time, the Golden One visited your dimension less. It was very sad because there was none to awaken the creative spirit in living things of colour and beauty. Colours and blooms began to fade; their size and perfume began to diminish. The royal guard fluttered helplessly, trying to do what the Golden One could, but they possessed not her magic touch. With time their colours began to fade also.

The coloured butterflies of old no longer exist. There are human beings who have never seen a butterfly; the moth has taken its place. The moth is a creature of dark shades. It is always drawn to the light. It is not an awakener or creature of beauty. Many are ugly, persistent, destructive creatures.

When the butterfly lays her eggs today she chooses a secret hideaway. She knows that to preserve colour and perfume of plant life, her offspring must survive. Only those who desire to give goodwill and loving service can see butterflies. Those who have selfish desires see moths.

As Man awakens to the spirit within he will create gardens of great beauty. Many butterflies will frequent these places. Man will be astonished by the splendour and glory of these gardens. They will be alive with living spirit.

The butterfly is a true creation of God. She reflects the magnificence and omnipotence of her Creator.

There are many social butterflies in human form today. These ones are attractive, colourful creatures. They flit from scene to scene but there is dissatisfaction with life in their hearts. They are selfish, superficial creatures. Their beauty is tarnished and only skin deep. They have little quality of soul.

The reason Butterfly was created was to reflect quality of soul. When there is soul quality there is clairvoyance. When there is clairvoyance, colours of greater brilliance can be seen because the spirit within is alive and actively creative. You might say: all this Man touches turns to gold. The greater the service one desires to give to one's fellow man, the more creative one becomes. When the service one gives awakens the living spirit within Man, that one is then of the vibration of the golden butterfly. This Man's garden will be a Garden of Eden because this Man's garden will see and experience the touch of the golden butterfly.

I am the Light of Butterfly.

PHOENIX

 AM THE LIGHT OF PHOENIX.

To humans the phoenix symbolizes rebirth. When one is reborn, one is born into light. In the time before time all creatures of Earth were immortal. They were conscious of the spirit within. They knew they were creations of a Creator, and they were eternal spirit.

When there is eternalness, there is no time. The Creator of All created that the immortal ones become mortal. When one is mortal, one loses spiritual consciousness. It was destined that all forget the truth of creation. As creations lost immortality and became mortal, time came into existence. With the coming of time came darkness or night. With the coming of darkness there came into existence death and fear of mortality. A mortal and immortal creature was created. That creature was called Phoenix.

Phoenix can be likened to an Earth creature, and also a heavenly creature. This creature actually did exist. He was a confused creature. He walked the Earth when time was coming into existence. He was of the vibration of immortality and mortality. Phoenix was a physical creature, and also a spiritual creature.

As darkness spread across the Earth Phoenix lost his immortality. He became mortal. He became so fearful that his life was one of torment and terror. He hardly knew what he was about. He was an agitated, lost soul. He longed to regain what he knew not. He was friendless and lonely.

By the time Phoenix lost all memory of his true vibration he had become an agitated, nervous creature. He feared what he could not see, and what he could see disgusted and caused him pain. Because all memory of eternal spirit had left him, he feared to die. When one fears death one's thoughts continually centre around death and dying. Fear generates fear and Phoenix's Earthly life was fearful. He despised living yet he was terrified to die. He had forgotten spirit is eternal and does not and cannot die.

The devolution of Phoenix symbolized the devolution of creation. All that devolves must, with time, evolve. The spirit sleeps while there is devolution. It awakens when there is evolution.

When Phoenix could bear no more fear, pain, torment, suffering, he literally threw itself into a heap and begged, for help. It was evident death was upon him yet somehow he knew his death was not to be. It was untimely. Instinctively he knew he was a living example of something and he was determined he would live and set an example for others to follow.

His fear began to fade. As it faded, so did his pain. He actually felt the spirit within himself awakening and burning up the negativity within. As it became more awake, active or living, he lost his fear of death. He slowly began to walk with confidence. All who had left him alone in his agony came to look and wonder at his recovery. They could not believe such a thing was possible. To mortals he had been beyond help. They'd believed he was beyond resurrection.

Phoenix knew he had undergone transformation of dark into light. He knew he had been born again and he wanted to share his immortality with others. When he tried to answer their questions, none would believe the spirit within him had awoken and healed him. He became quieter and quieter. His original exuberance of spirit settled into a state of eternal being, and he disappeared from the sight of those who refused to believe he was mortal and immortal.

This one can understand mortal suffering and he can understand immortality. Whenever it is time for a human to end Earthly life or suffering, Phoenix presents itself in some shape or form to take away the fear or pain of death. This one will gently lead another over the threshold into a life of change or physical death without fear.

Those who know Phoenix are blessed souls. Many in the past have not known of his existence and therefore could not be reborn. When there is rebirth, one is born into truth of spirit. With truth comes freedom from past suffering. Those who suffer and fear are the living dead. When the phoenix is in Man, Man transforms himself. The old Man or state of being dies and the new Man is born. When the living are reborn the angels in heaven rejoice. They rush to give service to this one.

All who witness the changed Man wonder at his transformation. Some wish to follow the example he sets; others turn away, believing not in what they see. The phoenix is unaffected. He is detached from the pain little ones inflict. His ego is non-existent. He knows transformation into light is only possible when it is time for the eternal spirit to evolve into wakefulness. It is this one which transforms darkness into light. It is this one which gives mortal Man immortality. It is this one which resurrects Man from death. It is this one which gives Man eternal life. This one is a spirit of eternity.

Because this spirit is in all life, life is continuous. The seasons of Earth come and go. The flowers die and come again. There is no death, there is but change. All things must change. When there is change, one is born into new experiences. It is the experiences of life which eventually lead Man to the phoenix.

Man, like the flowers, grows old and dies, but the seed of the flowers does not die. The flowers come again. The seed or spirit of Man is continually sprouting, living, dying as do the flowers. This is called reincarnation. Whilever Man is mortal or the spirit within is unaware of its immortality, Man remains on the cycle of birth, death, rebirth. He must return to Earth to evolve through time.

The phoenix operates only on Earth. When Man is reborn on Earth he becomes immortal. This does not mean the physical body cannot die. All mortal bodies die. They are affected by time. The immortal ones graduate from Earthly experiences. They transcend time and Earth.

There are many mortals walking Earth today. Their suffering is intense. Their imagination runs riot and they fear what they imagine. They are terrorized, tormented souls. Thoughts of death, torture and fear constantly accompany them. Phoenix is unknown to these ones. Those who know Phoenix watch and wait with patience. These ones are wise. They await the opportune time to give service to ones who regard them as their mortal enemies. Those who fear change or rebirth reject Phoenix. Time is forcing these ones to change; it is forcing evolution of mortality. The immortal ones stand by, as the angels in heaven stand by, waiting to rush to the aid of those struggling out of darkness into light.

When the time is right, Phoenix appears. He is present always at the time of rebirth. With love Phoenix takes the hands of lost ones and leads them on to the spiritual path. It can be a time of great pain for the mortal soul, but it is a time of great joy for the immortal one. This one agonizes with the other, but the agony is short-lived because Phoenix guides the other to the light.

Transformation in some occurs instantly. The greater the light within the guiding one, the quicker the transformation. It is love that awakens the eternal spirit in Man. The greater the love, the quicker the rebirth.

When one is born of the vibration of the phoenix, one is destined to experience the power of the dark. One is destined also to experience and effect change with the assistance of powerful, immortal, light beings. These ones become one with immortal Man. They manifest change for the highest good of all concerned.

The vibration of the phoenix, at this point in time, is rising. It is time for evolution. When the phoenix rises, spirit is awakened. The spirit within Man is awakening. It is time for rejoicing.

I am the Light of Phoenix.

Universe of One

 AM THE SPIRIT OF THE UNIVERSE OF ONE.

There was a time when all the planets, the stars, the moon, the sun, all the celestial ones were one star. I am the spirit of that star. I was a star of enormity. My magnitude of light was beyond the comprehension of humanity. The energy that I projected to other stars or universes was a creative energy. I beamed creative energy to other universes. These other universes were my family. We all beamed differing energies to the other and so the family of universes operated as a union.

I became discontented and dissatisfied with my creative energy. I wanted to experiment with creativity. To cut a long story short, I separated myself from my family. I discovered that it was not a wise thing to have done. Without their complementary energies I could not operate alone as I believed I could. I thought I could survive without the love my mother beamed to me, the wisdom my father freely gave me, the companionship of my siblings, and so on. I became a lost universe. My creative energy could not be released. There was none to receive it. I had totally separated myself from my source. I longed to create but creative energy must have a direction. I was a universe of creativity. It was my father who had the mind. I had to learn to think. In my endeavour I uttered a sound. That sound had a reaction. I exploded. I separated into myriads of pieces. My creative energy was scattered into many things. I discovered for every action there is a reaction when one has a mind. I became a universe of separate parts. All of the parts could do as I'd done because they all were part of me. What I did not anticipate in my experimentation with creative mind was that all things of my creation would self-destruct as I'd done, and so I created a plan to resurrect or restore myself.

I created that, with time, all my parts would create wholeness or oneness within themselves. As they did, my creative light would regain a little more of its former glory until eventually all parts of me returned home or back to their source of creativity. When that happens, I will return to my family, having grown in creative light.

In my plan of creation I created that each of my separated parts be able to experience self through another part of me. I created Man on Earth so that Earth herself could gain light. I created the animals to reflect Man. I created the birds, the trees, the flowers. I created all things to mirror or reflect truth. Without truth there is no light. If there is no light in my separated parts, I cannot regain magnitude. In my plan I created that my magnitude would be restored.

Because I am a separated universe, each of my parts is separate. I will confine myself to telling the story of Earth. Earth is a child or part of me. Earth is a planet of many people and animals. All these I created in likeness of myself. When I created Man, I created him whole, but because of my separation, he also had to create separation within. Original Man was hermaphrodite. He was sexless. As Man separated, he became two. He became a creator and he became a mind. He became female, he became male. This was not a comfortable state of being, and so one became two. Since that time Man has unconsciously striven to regain his separated part. Woman has longed to regain union but it could never be until it was time for all to gain truth.

There can never be unity, wholeness or oneness while there is separation. Whilever there is separation of the sexes, there is disharmony and disease on Earth.

In my original plan I created the return of all to its original state. It is time disharmony, uncooperation and discord ceased.

Back long, long ago when Earth began to create separation, countries became separated. Many drifted from the mainland. Some sunk, some survived. Australia was a survivor. Today its people know not they are of the stars. They have forgotten their own creation. They know not they are creators because they are part of me.

Throughout time the light within them has become dim, but it still exists. There is a way back to truth. It is through each other and the animals. I say to you, recognize the dark within yourself and turn that darkness into light. Recognize truth in the mirror of animals and humanity. This is part of my plan of creation.

As you grow in light, Earth will grow in light. As Earth grows in light, I grow in light. When all things of the Universe of One grow in light, there will be union of my separated parts. I will be whole. I will be one. This is part of my plan of creation.

Love was what I left behind. Love is the energy of the mother. One must leave the mother to grow in mind. The mind cannot love. Love is of the heart. The home is where the heart is. It is not until one becomes whole that one can return to the mother. When I return home, I will receive love. When all on Earth return home with truth or light is when they will receive love.

All must return to the mother wherever she is. Whilever there is separation from the mother there can never be peace. Earth is the mother of humanity. For there to be love on Earth, mothers must return to mothers. For there to be wisdom on Earth, fathers must return to fathers. For there to be light on Earth, all fathers, mothers, sisters, brothers must return home. When all return home there will be union. Opposition or separation of sexes will cease. Male and female will unite. Two will become one.

At this point in time there is confusion and separation in the hearts and minds of Australia's people. Indeed, this is so for all the people of Earth. At this point in time there is contradiction and disassociation between the sexes. The male is operating from the heart, the female from the mind, and there is much confusion and disintegration within both. This creates separation. There must be separation before there can be union. The male understands not the female. The female is insensitive to the male's feelings. All in time will be resolved. It is all part of the plan of creation.

I am the Spirit of the Universe of One.

About the Author

Ellie Adel
Written in 1993

Ellie Adel was born in 1935 at Kogarah, N. S. W., Australia. She was the eldest of four children. Her father was a railway employee, her mother a shoe machinist.

She became a stenographer after leaving public school at the age of fifteen. At nineteen she married a fitter and turner and by the age of twenty-five had three daughters. Neither Ellie nor her husband had any spiritual interest or belief.

Between the ages of twenty-eight and forty-eight, as well as coping with household chores, wife and motherhood, she held a variety of jobs, from waitressing, cooking, shop and factory assistant to bread-carting and owning her own garden nursery in an effort to one day attain the home of her dreams.

At the age of thirty-five she suffered a pulmonary embolism for which, at the time, there was no apparent cause. This was followed by years of negative sensitivity to prescribed drugs and struggling to relate to people who were insensitive to drug sensitivity. Most of the people were professionally trained. They were qualified to prescribe or administer drugs.

At the age of forty-five she began to seriously question hard work, money, heartbreaking relationships and inability to achieve life goals.

This led to the study of philosophy, astrology, numerology, graphology, reflexology, iridology, and many other means of raising consciousness. All led to the study of spirit and evolution of the soul.

At the age of forty-seven she was diagnosed with rheumatoid arthritis.

At the age of fifty, refusing further medical treatment because no longer could she tolerate the ill effects of prescribed drugs, she was admitted to hospital in excruciating pain, crippled and bedridden, totally zapped of life and completely unable to cope with living.

It was with the assistance of a loving, supportive family and, in the initial stages, a doctor who cared, that out of martyrdom and crucifixion came resurrection, and a new Ellie was born.

The reborn Ellie was unknowingly of the vibration of the Star of David. She had a burning desire to heal herself with minimal or no drugs. This was accompanied by a strong 'knowing' that she would be healed, but healing would be slow and at some future date she would share healing knowledge with others.

It took time for her to learn to walk again. It took time for her spent quality of life to return. During that time she gained a new perspective and appreciation of life. In her B. A. days (before arthritis) she had frivolously and flippantly taken life for granted.

She began to question life. She questioned its quality and inequality, and why some have it and some do not. She questioned pain, disease, and suffering.

It took time for many of her questions to be answered, and it took time for her shocked nervous system to adjust to the answers and how those answers came.

They all came written automatically through her crippled right hand. As truth of the life force or god within came, she realized it was simply pure, creative energy that followed the direction of the mind. She realized how she, in ignorance, had negatively created her own inner dis-ease and life disorder by negative thought. She began to consciously create or think with an aware mind, visualizing herself whole or healed and vitalized. Slowly her dis-eased body began to change; it began to transform or heal itself.

As transformation or change took place it was with greater shock she realized that creative living spirit and consciousness was within everyone and everything, that all were one or part of an evolving whole, but only human consciousness, at this point in time, was capable of evolving to this realization. She realized extermination of the human race, by the incredible power of its own negative thought and spiritual energy, was inevitable if individual human beings did not become aware of inner creative energy, and responsibly, and intelligently, create for the highest good of themselves and others.

Ellie believes she received her divine gift of inspired writing as a consequence of her deep desire to seek and gain truth and share that truth with others. She has faith, and is confident her fables will inspire and encourage others to initially create self then planetary and universal healing.

Ellie's Golden Fables is the first of three books to be published on healing by the self. Each fable in each book has been written with the specific purpose of raising consciousness or dispelling ignorance of the god force or inner creative life spirit.

The intention of every fable is to convey that ignorance is always accompanied by negative thought, self-will, disorder and dis-ease, and awareness is always accompanied by positive thought, goodwill, order and ease.

Ellie believes she is living proof that the inner creative spirit or life force, which some call God, and an enlightened mind can create healing and quality of life.

ABOUT THE ARTIST

Danielle Kluth
(Danielle wrote this and
did the illustrations in 1993)

Danielle Kluth was born into an artistic family in 1951 in Germany. Her father was an artist, her mother a potter.

Most of her childhood was spent in South Africa. She grew up as an only child in wild mountain country outside Cape Town with animals as her main companions and friends. This allowed her to cultivate a somewhat 'other-worldly awareness' which was deep-rooted in what today is known as 'Earth consciousness'. This facet of her nature was to become the most telling influence in her art and life in general.

At fifteen she left school in Stellenbosch, South Africa and spent seven months in a school in Germany, followed by two years' Art College in Lausanne, Switzerland. Returning to Cape Town, she continued to study art, and at twenty became apprenticed in her father's advertising agency. She later realized, when employed in other agencies and art studios, that the world of advertising with its hyper-pace, falseness and exploitation was not for her.

She met an Australian artist and went to Australia with him in 1973. During the seventies she did portrait painting in both Europe and Australia.

She returned to Australia and became active in various environmental movements. Any creative work done during that period of her life was on a voluntary, grassroots level, in keeping with her activist lifestyle.

With activist days behind her, Danielle spent three years working in a school with handicapped children. She is currently studying naturopathy.

She has a nineteen year old daughter, Natasha, who herself has a promising, artistic future.

Danielle lives at Maianbar, a south of Sydney suburb in the Royal National Park, with her partner Glenn who is a school teacher and Tai Chi instructor.